The Authentic Yoga

The Authentic Yoga

A fresh look at Patanjali's Yoga Sutras with a new translation, notes and comments

P.Y. DESHPANDE

RIDER AND COMPANY
London Melbourne Sydney Auckland Johannesburg

Rider and Company
An imprint of the Hutchinson Publishing Group
3 Fitzroy Square, London W1P 6JD

Hutchinson Group (Australia) Pty Ltd
30–32 Cremorne Street, Richmond South, Victoria 3121
PO Box 151, Broadway, New South Wales 2007

Hutchinson Group (NZ) Ltd
32–34 View Road, PO Box 40–086, Glenfield, Auckland 10

Hutchinson Group (SA) (Pty) Ltd
PO Box 337, Bergvlei 2012, South Africa

First published 1978
Reprinted 1980

Set in Monophoto Times
by Thomson Press (India) Ltd, New Delhi
Printed in Great Britain by The Anchor Press Ltd
and bound by Wm Brendon & Son Ltd
both of Tiptree, Essex

ISBN 0 09 133831 X

He, who sees this does not see death;
he sees neither illness nor suffering.
He who sees this sees all that is,
he attains everything everywhere.

Chandogya Upanisad, VII, 26, 2

Contents

Introduction 1

PART ONE SAMADHI PADA

1 The Discipline of Yoga 19
Sutras 1 to 4
Notes and comments

2 The Five-fold Vrttis 25
Sutras 5 to 11
Notes and comments

3 The Way to Vrtti-nirodha 32
Sutras 12 to 16
Notes and comments

4 Towards Samadhi 35
Sutras 17 to 22
Notes and comments

5 The Way of God-awareness 41
Sutras 23 to 29
Notes and comments

6 Impediments on the Way 46
Sutras 30 to 33
Notes and comments

7 The Alternative Ways 53
Sutras 34 to 39
Notes and comments

8 From Steady State to Reflecting State 60
Sutras 40 to 46
Notes and comments

9 From Seed-based to Seedless Samadhi 67
Sutras 47 to 51
Notes and comments

PART TWO SADHANA PADA

1 Yoga in Action 73
Sutras 1 and 2
Notes and comments
2 The Nature of Tensions 78
Sutras 3 to 9
Notes and comments
3 Pratiprasava – The Way Out 84
Sutras 10 to 17
Notes and comments
4 The 'Seer' and the 'Seen' 91
Sutras 18 to 25
Notes and comments
5 The Eight-Petalled Flower of Yoga (1) 98
Sutras 26 to 29
Notes and comments
Sutras 30 to 55
Notes and comments

PART THREE VIBHUTI PADA

1 The Eight-Petalled Flower of Yoga (2) 107
Sutras 1 to 3
Notes and comments
2 From Samadhi to Sanyama 115
Sutras 4 to 8
Notes and comments
Sutras 9 to 13
Notes and comments
3 The World of Yogic Reality (1) 122
Sutras 14 to 18
Notes and comments
4 The World of Yogic Reality (2) 129
Sutras 19 to 22
Notes and comments
Sutras 23 to 55
Notes and comments

PART FOUR KAIVALYA PADA

1 Nature and Man 141

Introduction

1

This book makes a fresh inquiry into and a new approach to the understanding of Yoga as it is expounded in Patanjali's Yoga Sutras. An explanation is needed for adding one more book to the vast literature available on the subject all over the world, in many languages.

First and foremost, no commentator, not even Vyasa, gives a precise answer to the basic question: what is Yoga?

Patanjali himself indicates the answer in the very title of his book: *Yoga Darsanam*. But there is no helpful comment on this title by any commentator. *Darsanam* or *Darsana* means looking at, seeing, observing; also knowing, understanding, perceiving; and also inquiry, examination.

Even traditionally speaking, just as Nyaya, Vaisesika, Sānkhya and Vedānta are *darsanas*, each with its own way of inquiry into and its own approach to reality, so also Yoga is a *darsana*, with its own approach to reality, based on its unique method of inquiry into the nature and structure of the world, and into man who looks at and finds his being in the world.

The traditionalists have generally denied the status of a *darsana* to Yoga. They somehow came to assume that Yoga was only a matter of practice, based on the Sānkhya vision of reality. And so it has been maintained traditionally that Yoga is not a *darsana* in its own right. The traditional name given to this misconception is Sānkhya Yoga. Because of this prestigious but misconceived view, Yoga has not received the attention it deserves. This small book is an attempt to remedy this defect and to make a fresh study of Yoga, as a *darsana* in its own right. That this is the right approach to Yoga is strengthened by the fact that Patanjali's book of Yoga Sutras makes no reference to any other *darsana*, not even to Sānkhya. Apart from the fact that he uses the words *purusa* and *prakrti*, terms which are also used by the Sānkhya *darsana*, his whole treatment of the world and man's relationship to it is unique and has nothing whatever to do with any other *darsana*. Even the basic Sānkhya terms, *purusa* and *prakrti* when they are used in the Yoga Sutras, carry meanings not wholly identical with the meanings given to them in the Sānkhya Darsana. And the three *gunas*, mentioned in Sānkhya as the innate attributes of *Prakrti* (Nature), *Satva, Rajas* and *Tamas*, are given three different names in Yoga Darsana. Here they are called *prakasa, kriya, sthiti*. These words carry meanings which cannot be equated with those given to *satva, rajas* and *tamas* in the Sānkhya Darsana.

However, it is not my intention to enter into controversy with the traditionalists. As a student of Yoga Darsana, it is clear to me that all controversies are utterly futile. I am concerned with only one thing; to inquire into afresh and understand *Yoga Darsana*, independently of any comparison with any other *darsana* or discipline.

2

The Yoga Sutras are statement of facts as they are seen in their existential authenticity. They can be so seen only after an independent and radical inquiry into the nature and structure of the existential situation. This ever present existential situation unfolds itself to us through the very act of pure seeing. This act of seeing is not man-made or mind-made. It springs from the very nature of man's being. When one's eyes are open one sees whatever there may be in the range of one's vision. One cannot wish it away. Wishful thinking or any form of ideation is irrelevant to the act of seeing. It is rather man, as an existential entity, who looks at what is there already in its existential majesty and immensity. At the one end of this existential situation is the 'Seer' and at the other end is the 'Seen'. The interaction between these two entities explodes into a vision (*darsana*). This vision is simply choiceless awareness of the totality of what is, in its existential authenticity. It is a vision untouched and untarnished by any mental activity.

The uniqueness of the Yoga Sutras lies in the fact that they take the primary act of looking at the world as the very foundation of Yoga Darsana (the vision of reality). Thus the act of seeing itself reveals the nature of the existential situation as a trinity of seer–seen–vision (*drasta–drsya–darsana*).

Each of these three components of reality is distinct from the other two. But this distinction springs from a clarity of vision which has nothing to do with the divisions of space and time. These divisions appear when ideation intervenes and usurps the place of pure seeing. These three integral components emerge as though out of nothing, as a result of the very act of seeing: they are not man-made or mind-made. The act of seeing is like the act of breathing. A man goes on breathing whether he is conscious of it or not. Breathing is an existential activity. To say 'I breathe' is ideational. Similarly, to see is an existential activity. But to say 'I see' is ideational. Actually, that which enables man to see, inquire, understand, is the 'seer' in the existential sense of the word. On the other hand, the sense of 'I-am-ness' or personal identity is a product of the past, which is totally unrelated to the living present in which reality abides. Reality 'is' irrespective of what man thinks, feels or does. But ideationally the sense of 'I-am-ness' usurps the place of the existential 'seer' and thus becomes the source of all manner of confusion. When one says, 'I am the seer or the observer', one implicitly includes in this 'I' one's body, senses and mind. But all these are capable of being observed either directly as in the case of the body, or through their operations, as in the case of the senses and the mind. They thus belong to the realm of the 'seen'. The sense of 'I-am-ness' is thus made up of the fusion of the 'seer' and the 'seen' (II-6). It is a concept born of confusion. The fact is that the energy that enables man to see (*drk-sakti*) and the energy that constitutes the 'seen' (*darsana-sakti*), including mental images and material objects or events, are two distinct energies which constantly interact with each other. They must never be confused with one another, nor are they interchangeable. If they were then perception itself would collapse altogether and everything would be reduced to an unintelligible chaos. This is why Yoga defines the sense of 'I-am-ness' (*asmitā*) as follows: 'To assume that the energy that enables one to see [*drk-sakti*] and the energy that constitutes the seen [*darsana-sakti*] are one and the same thing, is a tension called *asmita* [the sense of 'I-am-ness] (II-6).

Asmita is described as a tension (*klesa*) because it generates a contradiction between the what is, the existential, and what it is thought to be – the ideational. This tension comes into being as a result of inattention to and hence unawareness (*avidya*) of what from moment to moment actually is. This unawareness (*avidya*) is the soil, in which all other tensions take root (II-4). Not only this; it topsy-turvies man's vision of reality (II-5).

Yoga is thus an extraordinary state of being in which the choice-making movement of the mind comes to a standstill and one remains in a state of choiceless awareness of 'what is' (I-2). Although extraordinary, it is yet within the reach of every human being. It is extraordinary only in contrast to the ordinary conditioned state of being in which man is born and brought up. This conditioned state is maintained by the pressure of the prestigious norms of social conformity, but it can be challenged by the man who is willing to do so in the interests of discovering the truth which underlies his conditioned and conformist way of living. Such challenging demands freedom. Man knows that he has freedom to choose. But rarely does he raise the basic question as to what this freedom means and implies, Despite the fact that his identification with the results of his choices leads him repeatedly and inevitably into tensions, conflicts and misery. But anyone who cares to challenge this situation will be forced to raise the question: what after all is freedom? Is it restricted to choosing and then making man a victim of the relentless and vicious logic of choice-making? Or is there something more implied in the very nature of freedom? Does freedom to choose also imply freedom not to choose? It must necessarily be so. Otherwise the word freedom would lose its very meaning. It is this momentous discovery that has inspired the vision of reality, that is Yoga Darsana.

Freedom must mean freedom to choose, as well as not to choose. Not to choose is also to make a choice. But being negative it acquires an altogether new dimension. It does so because opting for not choosing ends, once and for all, man's identification with the choice-generated world of ideation, illusion and make-belief. It brings about a radical revolution in the conditioned way of life, in which man gets caught up. It resolutely rejects everything which belongs to the realm of the ideational and brings man face to face with the existential situation. Man, so brought face to face with the existential situation, is just a focal point of pure awareness. It is customarily designated as 'I' – a mere name, without any attribute, not even that of 'I-am-ness'. It is like a point which has position but no magnitude (*swarupa-sunyamiva*, III-3). It is a point on which all things converge and from which everything acquires a radiant significance.

This is what is meant by Yoga as described in I-2. Yoga is *citta-*

vrtti-nirodha – a state of being in which the ideational choice-making movement comes to a standstill. As is explained in the 'Notes and comments' that follow this introduction, this is a state that comes into being as a result of a man's exercising his innate freedom in the direction of 'not-choosing'. There is no egocentric control, no suppression or repression of thoughts or any kind of effort involved in this act of not-choosing. It is just a matter of exercising freedom in the right direction and of letting the existential situation reveal what it may, under the fiery gaze of pure perception.

It is unfortunate that all commentators, following Vyasa, have failed to understand the significance of the words *citta-vrtti-nirodha*, which are in fact consonant with the central theme of Yoga Darsana, which is freedom (*kaivalya*) from all bondages of conditioned consciousness. Therefore to opt for not choosing is to take the first and final step towards *kaivalya* (total freedom).

The first four Sutras state in a nutshell the very essence of Yoga Darsana. They tell us, in terms of an existential imperative, that man must opt for 'not-choosing' and exercise his innate freedom in this negative direction (*citta-vrtti-nirodha*) if he wishes to become established in his existential identity. The only other option open to him is to become entangled in identification with choices (*vrtti-sarupya*, I-4) and suffer the consequences of inevitable tensions, conflicts and misery which that entails. The existential situation offers no other alternatives.

3

Another contribution of great profundity and decisive significance which Yoga *Darsana* makes to the understanding of the existential situation is this: it draws a clear-cut distinction between a view or vision born of unawareness of what is (*avidya*), on the one hand, and a vision born of alert awareness of the inevitability of misery resulting from a stupid and dogged clinging to the sense of 'I-am-ness' and the motivations it generates, on the other. The former is called '*avidya-khyati*' (II-5) and the latter is called '*viveka-khyati*' (II-15 to 26). The word *khyati* means *darsana* or vision.

There are thus two kinds of vision to which Yoga Darsana draws our attention. The one is a legacy which lingers in man's mind and consciousness. It is given to man by the flow of nature (*Prakrtyapura*, IV-2), and is unconsciously strengthened by his cultural and social heritage. At the bottom of this lies identification with the forms which choices take.

Under the influence of this heritage man takes it for granted that he, as a product of nature, is totally separate from the objective, phenomenal world. He therefore believes that all he can do to understand this world and establish a meaningful relationship with it, is to pick and choose from it and subject it to a rational scrutiny by the method of trial and error.

Man therefore assumes that he has no option but to pick and choose and to train his inborn freedom to choose more and more rationally. But then it could be asked: what is reason? Reason could only be that which discards all gratuitous assumptions. And since at the root of all assumptions lies the sense of 'I-am-ness' – a product of conditioned consciousness, the reason that has fallen a prey to the assumption that the 'I' or the 'ego' is both the 'seer' and the 'chooser', must ever remain suspect. Therefore free inquiry alone, and not the effort of reason which has already been perverted by presuppositions, offers the only possible approach to the understanding of both internal and external reality. Such free inquiry is what underlies the Yogic approach to reality. To be in a state of free inquiry is to be in a state of choiceless awareness, which is the beginning of Yoga or meditation.

In the light of this it should not be very difficult to see that it is *avidya-khyati* that overwhelmingly dominates the scene of human life all over the world. This has been so throughout history, barring some lucid moments here and there. The fact that man still remains a victim of tensions, conflicts and chaos which repeatedly and inevitably land him in unrelieved misery, is proof enough that he has yet to discover a sensible and sure foundation for his approach to the existential situation.

A clear understanding of the Yoga Sutras offers a way out of this predicament. The notes and comments on the Sutras of Part II of the text deal with this problem. The points to be noted in this connection may be summarized as follows:

1. So long as man remains unaware of his inner tensions and finds no way out of their tentacles, there is no possibility of his ever coming face to face with the existential situation as a whole. And so long as tensions are allowed to have their way, all talk of progress and human welfare must remain utterly meaningless and repeatedly end up in despair and misery. All ideational and technological attempts to

escape from tensions and misery can only deepen the misery more and more because of the false hopes which they generate.

2. To see this predicament as a mind-made and man-made distortion of the existential situation, and to come face to face with it without trying to escape from it by any palliative, is to establish the first vital contact with reality. It is this contact with reality which itself unfolds the right way of understanding the real nature and structure of one's conditioned consciousness as being a product of tensions and of ideational ways of escaping from them.

3. The right way to free oneself from all tensions is the way of *pratiprasava*. This means a journey of exploration in reverse of going back from the peripheral surface tensions to their very roots. This is the way of meditation. In meditation one's mind remains stationary and only pure perception is allowed to operate on all the impulses emerging out of one's conditioned consciousness. Such is the probing and penetrative power of such perception that the impulses, as they arise, are seen in their true colours, with all their egocentric motivations. And because they are seen for what they really are, and because the mischief they are capable of doing is thoroughly understood, they disappear, once and for all, leaving the mind clean and crystal-clear.

4. It is out of such a purified mind that a penetratingly critical and sharply discerning intelligence (*viveka*) comes into being. It is this intelligence, which has its roots in the existential situation, that can distinguish and discriminate between the eternal and the ephemeral; the pure and the impure; and between happiness and sorrow. Because of such clear perception that never allows any scope for confusion, this newly born intelligence (*viveka*) destroys the vision born of *avidya* (II-5), once and for all. Clarity of vision now continually illuminates the existential scene without a relapse into *avidya-khyati*.

5. It is the clarity of vision born of intelligence (*viveka*), that enables one to see what is truly meant by the words 'seer' (*drasta*) and the word 'seen' (*drsya*) or the objective world. The 'seer' is just pure seeing energy. But because of his identification with the sense of 'I-am-ness', man tends to see everything through the veil of his past experiences (II-20). Thus the dead past overshadows the living present so completely that the very distinction between the 'seer' and the 'seen' gets utterly confused and man's vision becomes completely distorted. He then forgets that the 'seer' can never be the 'seen' and the 'seen' can never be the 'seer'. To confuse the two in this way is to lose clarity of vision and to invite endless trouble and misery.

The new intelligence (*viveka*) also discloses what exactly is meant by the word 'seen':

- *(a)* The energy that constitutes the 'seen' has three attributes, *viz.* inertia, movement and illumination; and this energy is wholly distinct from the energy that makes pure seeing possible, which constitutes the 'seer';
- *(b)* The seen is a compound of organic and inorganic matter; and
- *(c)* the *raison d'être* of the existence of the 'seen' is to offer experiences (*bhoga*) to the 'seer' and thereby help man (the experiencer) to liberate himself from all bondages (*apavarga*) (II-18).

Thus in the view of Yoga the 'seer' at one end and the 'seen' at the other end are co-extensive with the whole universe; and the existential interactions between these two embraces the whole mystery of life and the cosmos. The nature of this interaction is misunderstood by man so long as he keeps looking at the world and at himself through the screen of past experiences. And when the mischief this does to life is seen and understood, intelligence comes upon the scene and clarifies the vision. This vision born of *viveka* (intelligence) is called *viveka-khyati*.

6. It is therefore *viveka-khyati* that opens up the possibility of a new way of life called the 'Eight-fold way of life' (*astanga-Yoga*, II-29).

7. This 'Eight-fold way of life' unveils the mystery underlying the interaction between the 'seer' and the 'seen'. One then sees that the knowledge or understanding which is born of *viveka-khyati* is not accumulative but creative, is capable of comprehending everything in the right manner, and is devoid of temporal sequence (III-54).

It is pertinent to note in this connection that Yoga Darsana gives a special meaning to the word 'intelligence' (*viveka*). It has nothing to do with intelligence as this word is commonly and loosely used in everyday life. The word intelligence as it is commonly used means nothing but an egocentric cleverness, or a utopian extravaganza.

Again, it must also be noted that Yoga Darsana rejects all forms of so-called progress, or enrichment of the human mind and life, that are not rooted in *viveka-khyati*. On the contrary, anything man may do, even walking on the moon, will, in the absence of *viveka-khyati*, not advance him an inch towards the discovery of his existential identity.

It is this discovery which alone will enable him to transcend the tyranny of natural and social conditioning. It is only such transcendence or liberation that can establish man in a radically new way of living, in which he is always moving towards ever new creation and total freedom. It is only in this way that an era of creative cooperation between man and man, and man and nature can ever see the light of day.

4

For the purposes of this introduction, only one further point need be added. This point has relevance for the contemporary human situation. And without it the unique and immense contribution of Yoga Darsana to human understanding as a whole would remain woefully inadequate.

It is a point which deals with the precise nature of three interrelated things: mind, life and reality.

Part IV, the last Part of the text, deals with the mystery which surrounds what is deemed to be indicated by these three words. The following is a summary of what the Sutras in Part IV have to say about the matter, as the very essence of what has been expounded in the previous three parts.

1. First of all the objective world is seen as being a product of the flow of nature (*Prakrtyapur*, IV-2). This is on a par with the modern scientific view of the universe. Secondly, the occurrence of the mutation of species is also attributed to the same flow of nature. This also anticipates the modern scientific view of natural evolution of the species. The appearance of man on the world scene is thus a matter that belongs to the mystery underlying the mutation of species.

The Yoga Darsana goes further than modern science and raises the question: where exactly must we search for the source of the mystery that underlies this universe in which man finds his being? If you concentrate only on the 'seen', the observable material world, you will leave out of account the 'seer' who undertakes the search. Again, if you concentrate only on the 'seer' or man, you will ignore the external world. Therefore, say the Sutras, the starting point of the search for reality must be an inquiry into the nature of the existential interaction between the 'seer' and the 'seen'. It is this interaction that relates man to the world. And it is the interaction that explodes into a vision of what is, internally and externally.

Secondly, say the Sutras, it is man's vision of 'what is' that is decisive for the right approach to the mystery that is reality. This is so because man is the end-product of the mutational energy of nature. Mutation once brought about remains irreversible. The species other than *Homo sapiens* remain in their specific challenge–response patterns until they decay and become extinct. *Home sapiens* is the only species which carries with it the energy of being conscious of itself in its dynamic relationship with the world. It is as though the entire flow of nature or cosmic evolution becomes conscious of itself in Man. And it is the gift of language which enables man to be so self-conscious. Man alone can say 'I am I. I am not the other, and can never be the other'. It is this self-consciousness that distinguishes man from the rest of the animate and inanimate world. And therefore the source of the mystery underlying reality must necessarily lie in language and language-born self-consciousness. But language that enables man to be self-conscious cannot cross the frontiers of 'I am I, I am not the other, and can never be the other'. The use of language beyond the frontiers of this self-consciousness must ever remain inferential or imaginative. That is to say, it must ever remain ideational as distinct from the existential nature of self-consciousness. Therefore the search for the understanding of reality must be pinned down to a root-finding inquiry into the nature of man's self-consciousness. And since the conscious choice-making operations based on the brain–mind complex, lie at the bottom of any vision that man forms and clings to about himself and the world, the inquiry into the reality of things must further be pinned down to the nature and structure of the psyche of man. Man as the end-product of the mutational energy of the flow of nature must inquire and find out the right way of looking at himself and the world, to be true to his nature. He must find out when and how his view of what is, within and without, acquires the dimension of reality; and he must also find out what it is that interferes with and distorts the right view of reality. If man fails to do this, he must go the way of many an extinct species. And the whole drive and purpose of Yoga Darsana is to help man acquire a right vision of reality and thus save him from total extinction.

2. We have already seen how man, getting identified with his ideational choices, finds himself trapped in tensions, conflicts, chaos and misery; and how this *vrtti-sarypya* perpetually results in a distorted and unreal vision of the world, called *avidya-khyati*. And

we have also seen how a total awareness of the mischief that *avidya-khyati* does to human life flowers into a right approach to and an existential vision of reality, called *viveka-khyati*. The last part of the text carries the logic of *viveka-khyati* further and draws our attention to a clear distinction between a mind that is born of the impressions of accumulated experiences of the past which get activated by memory, on the one hand, and a mind born of Yogic meditation, which is free of the domination of the past or the known. The first is called *pratyayaja* or *pravrttija citta* (II-20; IV-3 to 5), and the second is called *dhyanaja citta* (IV-6), the meditational mind. The Sutras maintain that any inquiry into the reality of man and his living relationship with the world must begin with a root-finding inquiry into the human mind, with all its very subtle and baffling operations. This is so because it is these mental operations that motivate all kinds of human endeavour – secular, scientific, artistic, religious or mystic. The Sutras in Part IV give a detailed description of how the *pratyayaja* or *pravrttija citta* (the conditioned mind) operates and the kind of predicament it lands man in; and secondly, how *dhyanaja citta* (the meditational mind) operates and brings about a veritable mutational transformation of the conditioned mind.

3. The following is a summary of what the Sutras say about *pratyayaja* or *pravrttija citta* (conditioned mind):

(a) The human mind born of the flow of nature (*prakrtija citta*) is one and the same for mankind as a whole. This common human mind is a product of a mutational transformation brought about by the flow of nature. But this mutational quality of the mind gets distorted and the unity of this mind gets fragmented in individual minds. This happens because individuals tend to exercise their innate freedom to choose, to serve their petty egocentric ends, with which they get identified. They thus remain unaware of the vital dynamics of mutation which inhere in the human mind. They also remain unaware of the fact that man can neither originate nor maintain the flow of nature; and that all that is given to him is to avail himself of the existential flow of nature for the purpose of understanding himself and his relationship with the world. Because of this twofold unawareness of the existential human situation, individual human beings get trapped in egocentric choice-making and thereby go on

fragmenting endlessly the nature-made mind common to humanity as a whole. These fragmented individual minds differ from one another because of the differences in their egocentric choices. All these fragmented individual minds are the offsprings of the sense of 'I-am-ness' (IV-2 to 6).

(b) The actions (*karma*) of these fragmented egocentric minds take three forms: (i) bright, (ii) dark, and (iii) mixed. Neither of them spring from a vital touch with reality or the existential situation. Consequently these confused egocentric and ideational actions produce results in accordance with their own characteristics. They are grounded in the impressions of past experiences (*sanskara*), getting activated by memory (*smrti*). These impressions and the memory get fused into a complex, and become indistinguishable. In it the actual times and places of individual past experiences also get fused and thus become indistinguishable. In this way, that which has gone away (the past, the *atita*) and that which is yet to arrive (the future, the *anāgata*) both coexist in such conditioned minds. When such a conditioned mind encounters the living present, it responds to it in terms of the past which projects future expectations. The temporal matrix, made up of time viewed as unending sequences of past–present–future, thus comes into being. This mind-made temporality is projected on the external world, as though it belongs to the external world itself. The world is thus seen by the conditioned mind as a temporal order having causality as its motivating force. Causality presupposes a succession of moments, the earlier ones taken to be the causes of the later ones, *ad infinitum*. In reality, say the Sutras, time and causality are the projections of a conditioned mind on the external world. Remaining unaware of this fact, man gets trapped in a way of life rooted in temporality (made up of an unending sequence of past–present–future), in which the living present, the existential, becomes a perpetual casualty in every encounter with reality. This way of life is similar to the proverbial donkey perpetually chasing the carrot, which remains always beyond his reach (IV-8 to 10 and 12). It may be noted here that time as measured by the clock has nothing to do with temporality and causality as a mental fixation.

(c) What then is man to do? Sutra IV-11 answers the question. Man has to halt for a while, inquire and find out what lies

underneath his ideational and illusive way of life which perpetuates itself by never-ending hopes. One who does so inquire discovers that four factors lie underneath this conditioned way of living. These are: (i) motivations, (ii) results of these motivations, (iii) the supporting material produced by these results, and (iv) dependence on this whole process perpetuated by false hopes. A clear perception of each of these four factors operating as an unending chain of ideational reactions, gives an insight into the whole mystery of temporality. At the root of this temporality lies the beginningless actions (*karma*) triggered by built-in egocentric desires (*vasana*). They are called beginningless because the roots of these egocentric motivations and actions lie hidden in the dense darkness of the very origin of species, whose precise time and causation must ever remain a matter of sterile speculation (II-10).

Therefore, not speculation into the remote causes, but attention to 'what is' in the living present offers the only way out of the predicament of man. This attention, charged with the spirit of free inquiry, reveals that if man has freedom to choose, it is possible for him to exercise his freedom in negating the four factors that underlie his conditioned mind and the conditioned way of living. And when, by this method of attentive awareness, one gets established in the negative way of living and exploring, one succeeds in negating the domination of the complex of impressed past experiences and their memory. This negative way of inquiring and living empties the mind of all its contents. This is the way of meditation (*dhyana*). This brings about the death of the conditioned mind and the birth of a new mind, called *dhyanaja citta* (IV-6). The actions that emanate from this newly-born mind are neither bright nor dark nor mixed (IV-7). They are existential responses to the ever-changing situation, as distinct from the ideational reactions triggered by the memory of past experiences.

(*d*) This newly-born mind is free from temporality. The ways of a mind caught up in temporality are totally different from the ways of the mind which is born of meditation – a non-temporal state of being. This meditational mind does not more in any direction, past or future. It only reflects in purity the reality of the existential situation. Reality is that which remains one and the same throughout all changes. The new mind gets coloured by this reality. This is existential passion of the mind responding to reality. Reality thus becomes known, or remains unknown, relative to this existential passion (IV-14 to 17).

(e) This new mind, clear, calm and unmoving, reflects the 'seer' on one side and the 'seen' on the other. It is like the womb of a virgin capable of 'immaculate conception'. This conception results from the existential interaction between the 'seer' and the 'seen'. It is not of the nature of the mechanical action–reaction type. It is of a creative nature. It is called the movement of *pratiprasava* – a counter-creativity which is distinct from the blind procreative character of the flow of nature. This is a total fulfilment of, the *raison d'être* of, the very existence of man. It is not perfection or a static finality. It is the ending of the ideational sense of 'I-am-ness', on the one hand, and the beginning of man getting established in his existential identity, on the other. From now onwards man, a focal point of pure seeing awareness, moves with total freedom in harmony with the subtle and unseen movement of Cosmic Being. In this existential movement the three *gunas*, the three-fold energies that constitute the 'seen', offer their services to the creative energy of the 'seer' for ever-new creation. This creative energy is called *citi-sakti* – a word with which the Yoga Darsana comes to an end (IV-17 to 34).

Life is that which is endowed with this *citi-sakti* or creative energy. Pure-seeing awareness, that is man, operating through a transformed mind born of meditation, meets the three-fold energies of the 'seen' or the objective world, and explodes into ever new creation. Reality is this Radiant Creativity.

5

Yoga is a basic discipline, an essential prerequisite, for any religious, spiritual or mystic experience of Truth, God or Reality. Religion without a religious mind, is like a body without life or soul. A religious mind is a mind that has seen and understood the nature and structure of conditioned consciousness with all its ramifications, and that has, by the very act of understanding, unburdened itself of all its residue. It is a mind brought face to face with the existential situation, through man's opting for a new way of living, which is signified by the discipline of Yoga. Truth, God or Reality must ever remain mere words devoid of any substance or significance in the absence of Yoga and the clarity of vision that springs from it. Reality is not just 'what is'. It is a creative action that transcends 'what is'. Man without such transcendence remains a mere animal devoid of any awareness of '*that*' which animates all beings. Any analysis with the aid of any instruments, ideational or technological, will never throw any light on the analyser, the man. In the last analysis, it is man who is the measure of all things. And it is man with a mind that is the subject-matter of Patanjali's Yoga Darsana.

To write anything on Yoga Darsana is risky. It is made doubly so because of the Sutra way of exposition, in which it is offered by the great author. A *Sutra*, say the wise men of ancient times, is that way of communication in which a truth of universal significance is compressed into the fewest possible words, with crystal pure clarity which remains untarnished by the ravages of time. This, perhaps, is the reason why Patanjali never thought of adding any commentary or explanatory notes to the Yoga Sutras. The Sutras, therefore, are meant to be meditated upon rather than commented. This small book is the result of years of meditation, with the Sutras as the starting points. Its main drive is to draw pointed attention to the central theme of the Yoga discipline, which is perception of the truth underlying man's being and his way of living. If the book conveys what it was intended to do, it may then be put aside and the readers may be left to their own meditation to discover the hidden wonders of Yoga, to which there never can be an end. The authentic Yoga is a self-correcting and eternally creative discipline, with infinite potentialities.

What follows this introduction is a fresh translation of the Sutras, along with brief explanatory notes and comments. The text is divided by Patanjali himself into four Parts. Part I and Part IV are complete in themselves. Those who get the essence of Yoga through a meditational approach to either of them can easily anticipate what is expounded in Parts II and III. These are meant to help those who get the feel of what is contained in Part I, but nevertheless keep relapsing into the conditioned ways of thinking and living.

To facilitate understanding, the Sutras in each Part are sub-divided into small groups, each group elucidating a point, as though it were a milestone on the long and arduous path of Yoga.

A word about the title of this book. The word 'Authentic' in the title may sound rather provocative. But it is not used in that sense at all. It is used to indicate the astounding originality of Patanjali's approach to Reality, which carries with it the perfume of existential authenticity. The roots of Yoga lie hidden in the deep insights of the ancient Vedic seers. But here, in the Yoga Sutras, we distinctly hear its authentic voice. Hence the title *The Authentic Yoga*.

I end this introduction with a sense of gratefulness to a few friends for helping me in many ways. They would prefer to remain anonymous in the interest of Yoga. Even to give a name for the author of this book has no special meaning. It is a concession to social conformity, for which he begs to be excused.

P. Y. DESHPANDE

PART ONE
Samadhi Pada

1
The Discipline of Yoga

SUTRAS 1 TO 4

1. *Atha Yogānuśāsanam*

And now, the discipline of Yoga . . .

2. *Yogaścittavṛttinirodha*

Yoga is that state of being in which the ideational choice-making movement of the mind slows down and comes to a stop.

3. *Tadā drasṭuh svarūpevasthānam*

Then [when the movement of the mind comes to a stop] the seer gets established in his existential identity.

4. *Vṛttisārūpyamitaratra*

In all other states of being, identification with the ideational choice-making movement reigns supreme.

NOTES AND COMMENTS

These four Sutras give us the very quintessence of Yoga. They tell us about the basic requirements of the discipline that is Yoga – *Yoganusasanam.*

The word *anusasanam* is derived from the root *sas* with the prefix *anu. Sas* means to teach, instruct.* And *anu* means: to go along with. To go along with the teaching of Yoga is to learn about Yoga. A certain discipline, an attentive austerity, necessarily accompanies learning. One cannot learn anything without attention. And attention implies quietude and freedom from distraction. Unless one is in

*For the meanings of the Sanskrit words used in the Sutras the dictionary relied on mostly was *The Sanskrit–English Dictionary* by V. S. Apté, now brought out in three volumes and sponsored by the Government of India.

such a state of mind, learning would not be possible. This is the first requirement for the discipline of Yoga.

But sustained attention is not easy to come by. And without it one cannot go along with the teaching of Yoga. Therefore, something more is demanded. This 'something' is suggested by the very first word *Atha*. *Atha* means the beginning. Tradition attaches a further meaning to this word. They say that the word *atha* is used at the beginning of any work to invoke auspiciousness. But we are not talking to the traditionalists. We are talking to 'man' as a human being, irrespective of his antecedents. This is exactly what the Yoga Sutras do.

Literally translated, *atha* means: 'and now', or 'here now'. 'Now', or 'and now' or 'here now', presupposes something that was before this moment 'now'. What was before, up to this moment 'now', must end for learning the 'new' with which one is now confronted. This 'new' is Yoga. It demands a total break with the past, as would be evident as we go along with the Sutras. It is as though one has already gone through the various disciplines – social, scientific, moral, philosophical, religious – and, at the end of it all, one finds oneself in a state of total disillusionment. One thus comes to be in a state of not-knowing. It is this that is implied by the word *atha*. It is only when one finds oneself in such a state of not-knowingness, in which the past has become meaningless and the future poses an eternal question-mark, that one may possibly be able to maintain a watchful state of attention necessary to learn the new, that is, Yoga. And this is the second requirement of the discipline of Yoga, indicated by the word *atha*.

The nature of the past that becomes meaningless in this state is described in Sutra 4. *Vrttisarupya* (identification with the ideational choice-making movement of the mind) represents the totality of the past. If one still retains some hangover of the past which projects hope in the future, one will never be able to establish a meaningful contact with Yoga.

In Sutra 2, Yoga is equated with three words: *citta, vrtti* and *nirodha*. None of these words are defined or explained in the Sutras. In such a case one has to find out the right meanings of these words that are consistent with the central theme of Yoga.

The word *citta* is derived from the root *cit* which means 'to see, observe, perceive'. *Citta* is the past passive participle of the verb *cit*. It, therefore, means 'the seen, the observed, the perceived' – that is, that which has been experienced in the past.

The word *vrtti* is derived from the root *vrt* which means 'to choose, like'. *Vrtti* thus means the form which one's choosing takes.

The word *nirodha* is a compound of *rodha* with the prefix *ni*. The word *rodha* is derived from the root *rudh* which means 'to obstruct, arrest, stop'. And the prefix *ni* means 'slowing down'. *Nirodha* therefore means the slowing down of the choice-making movement of the mind (*cittavrtti*) and its eventual stopping by itself.

None of the commentators have cared to find out the root meanings of the words *citta*, *vrtti* and *nirodha*. They have followed Vyasa, who in his turn, followed the traditional or conventional meanings. But the fact is that Yoga rejects words with their traditional or conventional meanings. It even rejects past experiences and their verbalizations (I-15). Therefore, not conventional but root meanings have to prevail so far as these words are concerned which are used in the Sutras but not defined or explained in them.

Since the word Yoga is equated with *citta-vrtti-nirodha*, the precise way in which these words have to be understood becomes a matter of supreme importance. This cannot be left to the sweet mercies of any commentator.

The Yoga Sutras use the roots *vr* and *vrt* both of which means 'to choose'. The word *vrtti* also means choosing, along with other meanings not relevant to Yoga. In Sutra 3 of Part IV the word *varana* is used which also means 'choosing'. Choosing necessarily implies freedom. But to choose and then get identified with choices is to confine freedom to an activity triggered by past impregnations on the mind or the brain cells. Freedom to be real and meaningful must not be determined by the past.

Freedom from the already known the past, is the third requirement for right understanding of the discipline of Yoga. Freedom from the known, the past, implies freedom from ideational choice-making. To choose is to indulge in ideation. Choosing presupposes a selection between two or more alternatives presented by the factual situation. Actually, the factual situation presents nothing but facts. Not 'alternatives' but only 'facts'. It is the mind (*citta*) conditioned by the past and structured with built-in likes and dislikes, that wavers when confronted with a new situation. It is this wavering of the mind that triggers ideation, which refers back to built-in likes and dislikes. And it is this ideational choice-making tendency that indulges in selecting such aspects of the whole factual situation as correspond with its built-in likes, and in rejecting or ignoring those which correspond with built-in dislikes. This preference for the most likeable and rejection of the unlikeable constitutes the choice-making activity of the mind. This is always based on memory or the remembered past.

Freedom from the past, therefore, means nothing else than freedom from ideational choice-making. Choice-making itself presupposes freedom to choose. But this freedom gets vitiated by the remembered past which holds the mind in bondage – the bondage of built-in likes and dislikes. Therefore, freedom to be real, existential and meaningful must necessarily imply not only freedom to choose but also freedom 'not to choose'. The action of freedom imprisoned in perpetual choice-making is action gone wrong. It is an action that negates freedom, which initially gave birth to it. And freedom is the very breath of life. Caught up in perpetual choice-making, modifying it, from time to time to pamper to his petty likes and dislikes, man finds himself imprisoned in a self-made predicament from which he finds no escape.

Modern man is painfully aware that every action based on choice negates itself, every profound idea gives rise to another refuting it, and that every revolution leads to inevitable counter-revolution. The question is: is there any action which will not negate itself? Yes, says Yoga. It is a negative action of not-choosing. If there is freedom which enables man to choose, this very freedom must also enable him 'not to choose'. Freedom would be meaningless if it is to remain imprisoned in choices *adinfinitum*, landing man inevitably in conflict, chaos and misery.

Therefore, says Yoga, cease to choose and *see* what happens. Just as a wooden wheel keeps moving on so long as it continues to receive pushes from behind, so also the ideational choice-making movement of the wheel that is mind will keep on moving so long as the choices of man continue to operate as pushes from behind. On the other hand, just as a wooden wheel in motion will begin to slow down and eventually come to a stop by itself if the pushing is halted, so also if man ceases to choose, the wheel of the mind will naturally slow down and come to a stop.

This is what the word *nirodha* implies. It does not mean and imply a wilful control of *vrttis*, or their suppression or repression. Wilful control, suppression or repression must necessarily result in a derangement, if not the destruction of the psyche. Because any egocentric act of a man, already caught up in *vrttisarupya*, which has conditioned his mind, will be tantamount to exercising his freedom in the same old way, that is, choosing. This can never bring about *nirodha*, but only the death of the psyche if the pressure of wilful control, suppression or repression is persisted in beyond the point of endurance. Consequently, as the root of the word *vrtti* suggests, the only alternative open to man is to exercise his freedom for a change, in not-choosing. After this action of not-choosing, the past propelled wheel of mind will begin to slow down and naturally come to a stop. This is *nirodha* in the Yogic sense.

What happens when man *sees* the truth and falsehood involved in choice-making, and decides not to choose in the light of this new perception? Says Sutra 3, 'the seer gets established in his existential identity'. What is this existential identity (*svarupa-pratistha*, indicated by *svarupe-vasthanam* in Sutra 3)? Man, according to Yoga, is no more than a pure seeing entity (II-20). But, conditioned by the past, he tends to *see* through experiences. Experience is always of the past. When confronted with a factual situation, man turns the pure act of seeing into an egocentric act of experiencing, triggered by the remembered past. He must place what he sees, here and now, in the pattern of recognition built up by past experiences, painful and pleasurable. This placing of what is being seen, here and now, into the pattern of recognition, which is always structured by the past, is to see through the coloured and curved glasses of past experiences. This is distortion of 'pure seeing' and hence alienation of man from his existential identity (*svarupa*). It is distortion and degradation of the *existential* in favour of the *ideational.*

Sutra 4 sums up this distortion and degradation of the 'human' in man in one word, *vrttisarupya.* When man slips from existential seeing into ideational choosing he lands himself in *vrttisarupya*, generating tensions, conflict, misery and chaos. On the other hand, when man, realizing in all humility that he knows nothing about life and reality opts for not-choosing, he tends to remain established in his existential identity, flowering of itself into total freedom and creativity. In either case it is, initially, exercise of freedom. To exercise freedom in the direction of choice-making is to be experience-oriented and remain imprisoned in the past. On the other hand, to exercise freedom in the direction of not-choosing is to be seeing-oriented, or perception-oriented, and this tends towards getting one established in a timeless dimension. In either case it is, initially, a *cittavrtti.* The only difference is that in choice-making triggered by the past, the movement of *vrttis* invariably results in tensions, ending up in endless misery; whereas, in opting for not making choices, the movement of *vrttis* tends to slow down and get liberated from all tensions, and eventually dissolves itself in a quietude of total freedom and perceptive action, which is creation.

Basically, it is all a question of identity getting alienated from itself, or getting established in itself. Yoga points the way to the latter. Yoga, as it were, seems to whisper in the ears of man: Opt freely for the discipline of Yoga, or get finished as *Homo sapiens* from this beautiful earth.

2
The Five-fold Vrttis

SUTRAS 5 TO 11

5. *Vṛttayah pañcatayyah kliṣṭākliṣṭāh*
Vrttis are five-fold, painful and painless.

6. *Pramāṇa-viparyaya-vikalpa-nidrā-smṛtayah*
The five-fold vrttis are: proof-based knowledge; illusion-based knowledge; word-based knowledge; sleep-based knowledge and memory-based knowledge.

7. *Pratyaksānumānāgamāh Pramāṇāni*
Pramanas [forms of proof-based or valid knowledge] are of three kinds: direct sense knowledge, inferential knowledge, and knowledge based on the authority of scriptures (*agama*).

8. *Viparyayo mithyājñānama-tadrūpa pratiṣṭham*
Viparyaya is false or illusory knowledge based on seeing things having no existence in fact.

9. *Śabdajñananupātī vastuśhūnyo Vikalpah*
Vikalpa is knowledge based on words, which are devoid of reality.

10. *Abhāyapratyayālambanā-vṛttirnidrā*
Sleep is knowledge based on the experience of absence of things.

11. *Anubñutaviṣayasaṁpramoṣah smṛutih*
Memory is non-destruction or non-removal of the objects experienced in the past.

NOTES AND COMMENTS

Every movement of mind, or the arising of any ripple on the still waters of the mind, is a *vrtti*. *Vrtti* is mind in interaction. *Vrtti* is the source of all experience and knowledge. In fact *vrtti*, knowledge and experience are just shades of one and the same thing. Initially, at some point of time unknown to man, mind came into being as a product of the evolutionary movement of nature. This natural mind-stuff is common to all sentient species which all differ from one another. But members of each species (*jati*) have a common mind. Their responses to interaction with nature are of a uniform type. At a later stage of evolution man appeared on the scene. He evinced a natural tendency to utilize nature for his own ends, as a farmer utilizes the flowing water of the natural river by digging a canal from the river-bed to irrigate his fields (IV-3). This was the beginning of the emergence of an individualized mind in contrast to the herd instinct of other sentient species. In *Homo sapiens* the natural mind-stuff common to all men began to be split up into individual minds in accordance with the choice-making tendency operating in each individual. These man-made individualized minds were, and still continue to be, the products of the sense of 'I-am-ness' common to all individuals (IV-2 to 5).

This description of how different individual minds came into being is obviously based on the vision (*darsana*) of Yogis who had seen the necessity of freely opting for the negation of choice-making, and thereby came to have a mind qualitatively different from all other individual minds. This new mind, emerging in the Yogis, is named as *dhyanaja citta*, mind born of meditation. This new mind was seen to be devoid of the three kinds of activities – bright, dark and mixed up – common to all men who have not opted for the discipline of Yoga (IV-6, 7, 8).

The nature of the five-fold *vrttis*, now under discussion, has to be understood in the light of this extraordinary vision of Yogis. In this connection it may appear rather strange to many as to how sleep (*nidra*) can be called a *vrtti*, which is described as a form which choice-making takes. Choice-making is a voluntary act of mind or consciousness and, as such, cannot apply to sleep which is supposed to be involuntary, and in which one remains unconscious of everything, including one's own self. If the vision of Yoga is to be taken as authentic, then it would appear that a qualitatively new and a wholly radical mind (*dhyānaja citta*), which the discipline of Yoga brings into being, is a mind eternally wide awake, alert and so delicately and penetratingly sensitive that it sees through and cuts across all that the individualized and divided mind-stuff of men in general may ever hope to see. In such a Yogic mind sleep becomes a matter of choice. I have personally seen a few men who go to deep sleep in a matter of seconds and wake up at the appointed time. Consequently, the description of *vrttis*, and of all other connected matters appearing in

Yoga Sutras, has to be related to the vision of Yoga (Yoga Darsanam). And this vision is not a màtter to be taken on trust or on the authority of Patanjali or other Yogis. It is on the other hand, a matter of experimenting with *citta-vrtti-nirodha* and finding out the truth or otherwise of this Yogic vision. This is what the Yoga Sutras tell us with precise details.

Sleep or slumber (*nidra*) is, therefore, a *vrtti* embedded in the brain cells or in the mind-stuff circumscribed in individual consciousness and forming part of what is called the unconscious layer of the mind. The choice-making is thus both conscious and unconscious. Habit gets built into the psyche and its operation seems to be automatic rather than conscious. Along with the 'code' that is carried along from generation to generation by the human organism, the tendency to experience the absence of all things is also carried along, forming part of the inherited code. Sleep is thus a slumbering consciousness experiencing the absence (*abhāva*) of all things experienced in the waking state. It is not absence of consciousness, forming part of *citta*, but absence of objects experienced in the waking state. It is because of this fact that this experience of *abhāya* is capable of being remembered. If it were not an experience it could never have been recalled by the mind.

Memory (*smrti*) is a record of past experiences. And since every experience is an egocentric response to what is being seen, that is to say, it being a product of the built-in choice-making propensity, memory or remembrance of what has been experienced in the past, is also a *vrtti*.

Vikalpa is a very peculiar and a very important *vrtti* which has far-reaching consequences. Words are supposed to have meanings corresponding to the objective things which they indicate. But the fact remains that words are not things. The *word* dog is not the *animal* that is named as dog. But the power which the word exercises on the human mind is so great and has got so deeply rooted in the psyche that man has come to believe that the word is a source of objective knowledge. Actually, word-generated knowledge is devoid of any substance or objective reality. Words such as God, religion, *atma, brahma,* self, and so on, appear to conjure up images which in fact have no foundation in the objective world. And yet to the conditioned mind of man these words convey knowledge of meanings as though they were objective realities and few men, if any, can get over this belief, or rather prejudice. Experience of the thing called 'dog' is not on the same footing as experience of the thing called 'self'. This latter experience or knowledge is devoid of any reality, says the Sutra defining *vikalpa*.

There are a number of words which exercise such an enormous influence on the minds of men that they can hardly be brought to see the fact that all word-generated knowledge is devoid of any substance or reality. As we shall presently see, all word-generated *vrttis* have to be brushed aside, lock stock and barrel if one is to be able to see the truth or the reality of anything.

Viparyaya is a *vrtti* which also has enormous influence on the minds of men. To describe men as Hindus, Muslims, Buddhists, Christians, or as Indians, Chinese, British, French, Americans or as communists, socialists, democrats, and so on, is to mistake a human being for the labels given to him. This is *viparyaya*. And this is by no means as innocent and harmless as mistaking a piece of rope for a snake, which is the classic example of *viparyaya*. This false or illusory knowledge forms such an important part of human consciousness that it has now acquired the respectability of true and factual knowledge. This is knowledge by the back door. Openly, many will admit that these are examples of false or illusory knowledge. But few will act on this admission in their daily living. These and many other labels are always masquerading as 'objective realities' in the practical and psychological affairs of men all over the world. Labels as marks of recognizing pieces of luggage have a definite utility. But when men are recognized by the labels given to them, this *vrtti* results in disastrous consequences for the survival of human life as a whole on this planet. *Viparyaya*, as a *vrtti* embedded in the psyche of man, may well spell his doom.

Pramāna is the most respected *vrtti* in human life. Most of the scientific, philosophical, cultural and social affairs of men are governed by this *vrtti*. This *vrtti* demands proofs for the validity of any statement men may be inclined to make. Sense data, valid inferences in accordance with the norms established by the science of logic, and the words enshrining the wisdom of the sages, are the three components of this *vrtti*. It is a *vrtti* which examines its own validity in accordance with commonly accepted standards. But this *vrtti* is confined to so few and its influence on the minds of men in general is so slight that, despite its great contribution to the evaluation of value judgements, its power to bring under control the rampant irrationality and utter irresponsibility of the vast majority of mankind has repeatedly proved to be very feeble in human history.

The solid contribution to valid knowledge made by the *pramāna vrtti*, although important in many ways, remains limited to the understanding of the physical nature of the world. It is limited to objects, the observed (*drsya*), and excludes the observer (*drastā*) from its view. It fails to see the fact that no world-view could be valid unless the nature of the right relationship between the observer and the observed is discovered. Again, its approach to the objective world is confined to the discovery of the nature of the relationship between object and object in a fragmentary way, neglecting the requirement of ecological balance in the cosmos. This has already resulted in disastrous consequences. Yet another important point to be taken into account is that even in the limited field where this *pramāna vrtti* operates, the most important discoveries are not the products of this *vrtti*, which are confined to the pre-established norms of valid thinking, but of that intriguing something called intuition, inspiration, insight or a sudden flash of perception. Consequently, the credibility of knowledge obtained through this *vrtti* always remains not only limited but suspect even in its limited field.

And last but not the least, as an instrument of establishing intelligent and harmonious relationship between man and man, and man and nature, the entire accumulated contribution of this *vrtti* is already proving to be disastrous for the very survival of man on this planet. The combined threat of a nuclear holocaust, increasing global pollution and problems created by the population explosion, is forcing intelligent and compassionate men all over the world to halt for a while and take a fresh look at man's approach to existence as a whole. It is this halt and a fresh look that are implied in *citta-vrtti-nirodha*. Yoga therefore suggests a halt to the operation of all the five-fold *vrttis* so that man may place himself in a position in which alone perception of 'what is' within and without, with its existential significance for human life, would become possible.

Human life, as it has been lived ever since man passed from the animal to a cultural state, has been wandering within the vicious circle of these five-fold *vrttis*, none of which can ever succeed in bringing man face to face with himself or the world in which he finds his being. On the contrary, identification with these *vrttis* obscures that clear perception which alone can enable man to see things as they are in reality.

These *vrttis* are of two kinds: painful and painless (I-5). Naturally, existentially they need not become painful. They become painful only when choice-making ideation intervenes and distorts perception. This happens because there is an inherent contradiction between the ideational and existential. The pain and misery which the ideational processes engender assume such enormous proportions that man finds it impossible to discover a way out of their tentacles. Every way out, invented by the ideational movement, generates its opposite. This is inevitable because of the inherent contradiction between the ideational and the existential.

The very perception of this contradiction halts the painfulness of these *vrttis*. Because this perception brings man face to face with reality and brings home to him the necessity and urgency of opting for *citta-vrtti-nirodha*. When this happens, the past-propelled momentum of these *vrttis* naturally slows down. As a consequence, the nature and structure of these *vrttis*, along with their hidden motivations, are revealed to the 'seer'. This revelation helps man to walk out of the complex and confusing labyrinth of identifications. When man thus steps out of the past, he becomes free to use these *vrttis* as instruments for new discoveries. That is to say, *vrttis* remain painful only so long as their operations remain imprisoned within the closed frontiers of *vrttisarupya*. On the other hand, these *vrttis* become painless, and many even become effective instruments of new discoveries, when they become seeing-oriented (*khyati-visaya*) or perception-oriented, as opposed to ideation-oriented. All ideation is basically egocentric (*asmita-matra*) and, as such, creates a circumference of *vrttisarupya* (identification) all around, in which man is held a prisoner. This is what is indicated by the statement in Sutra 5 that '*vrttis* are either painful or painless'.

It is pertinent to note here that each of these five *vrttis* is distinct from the other four, *Pramāna* is not *viparyaya* and the rest. And *viparyaya* is not *pramāna* and the rest. But *smrti* (memory) is all-inclusive. It includes previous memories of all these five *vrttis*. One may forget a thing and remember it again. Therefore memory becomes the matrix of *vrttisarupya* (identification), which, in fact, is the matrix of temporality. It is in this matrix that man (perception incarnate) gets entangled and lost to his existential identity. As so lost, he responds to the challenges of circumstances and ever new situations from the matrix of memory-impregnations (*samskar*) in which he is held a prisoner. Disentanglement from this matrix of temporality, dominated by the past and past-propelled future, is freedom (*apavarga* or *kaivalya*). And freedom is the be-all and end-all of Yoga.

The way in which this disentanglement may be brought about is named as *citta-vrtti-nirodha*. This *vrtti-nirodha* is the basic condition for freedom and the perception of things as they are – that is, perception of truth or reality. The following Sutras give us a precise exposition of *vrtti-nirodha*.

3
The Way to Vrtti-nirodha

SUTRAS 12 TO 16

12. *Abhyāsavairāgyābhyām tannirodhah*
The slowing down and eventual stopping of *vrttis* becomes possible through *abhyasa* and *vairagya*.

13. *Tatra sthitau yatno-bhyāsah*
The energetic interest in attempt to remain in the stand-still state (*nirodha*) is called *abhyasa*.

14. *Sa tu dīrghakāla-nairaṁtarya-satkārāsevito dṛḍhabhūmih*
Persistence in this *abhyasa*, regardless of the passage of time, without interruption, and with an attitude of reverence, results in a firm foundation for Yoga.

15. *Dṛṣṭānuṣravikaviṣaya-vitṛṣṇasya vaśīkāra sañjñāvairāgyam*
Loss of craving for all that has been experienced in the past and for all that has been heard in the past results in *vairagya* which is also termed *vasikara*.

16. *Tatparaṁ puṙuṣakhyāterguṇa-vaitṛṣnyam*
Loss of craving for the *gunas* [the three-fold energies of the phenomenal world] resulting in man's seeing himself as he is [distinct from the operation of *gunas*], is called *paravairagya* [the ultimate or the supreme disentaglement from all bondages].

NOTES AND COMMENTS

We have seen that *vrttis* are of two kinds, painful and painless (I-5). *Vrttis* become painful as a result of one's identification with them (*vrttisarupya*, I-4). Identification is entanglement with *vrttis*. Non-identification results in disentanglement. Opting for 'not-choosing' results in non-identification. When choosing ceases, the momentum of past, impregnated *vrttis* slows down. This process of the slowing down of *vrttis* results in gradual disentanglement from them, because, having ceased to choose, one becomes a mere onlooker of *vrttis*. To be a mere onlooker is to be a 'seer' (*drasta*). When one remains a mere 'seer' one sees that *vrttis* (born of past impregnations) appear, stay for a while, and disappear. And then a stage comes when one sees that the disappearance or absence of *vrttis* continues for a while. This interval devoid of *vrttis* is called *sthiti* – a standstill state. This is an entirely new 'happening', not of a phenomenal nature (in which the continuity of events remains unbroken), but of an altogether different order of being. And because of this extraordinary 'happening', there comes about an energetic interest in this *sthiti* – an interval devoid of *vrttis* and, therefore, of time. This energetic interest in *sthiti* is called *abhyasa*.

Persistence in this *abhyasa*, as stated in Sutra 14, results in laying down a firm foundation for Yoga.

Thereafter, this persistence in *abhyasa*, a state in which one is a mere onlooker (seer), brings about a loss of craving for all that one has experienced or heard in the past. Such a loss of craving or appetite for objects of experiences and objects indicated by words, is in fact a disentanglement from identification with *vrttis*. Such a state of disentanglement is called *vairagya*.

But disentanglement from *vrttis* is one thing, and disentanglement from the three-fold energies (*gunas*) underlying the phenomenal world, is quite another, because these three-fold energies or *gunas*, are constantly operating within one's psychosomatic being. One's psychosomatic organism functions the way it does because of the operation of these *gunas*. The perception of this fact disentangles the 'seer' from *gunas* also. Such extraordinary perception implies total disentanglement of the 'seer' from the entire phenomenal world. There is now only 'pure seeing' of the phenomenal world, along with the three-fold energies which keep it perpetually going. Such 'pure seeing' is also an energy; but it is distinct from the three-fold energies or *gunas* of the phenomenal world. This 'pure seeing energy' is called *purusa*. This is Man in his existential authenticity. It is this perception that is called *purusa-khyati* in Sutra 16.

Khyati means *darsana*, seeing-awareness, as distinct from consciousness born of psychic entanglement with the entire phenomenal world. Man's body, his human organism, is a product of *prakrtyapur*, the flow of Nature. If the human organism did not carry with it something other than the *gunas* underlying the phenomenal world which includes the human organism, man would never be *aware* of either himself or the world in which he finds his being. This awareness is 'pure seeing' (*drsimatrata*, II-20). And it is this 'pure seeing' that is called *drsta*, 'seer', in Yoga.

Man and the world present a baffling complex that defies comprehension. Man as the observer, trying to understand the observable world, must first unravel the mystery that underlies the observer–observed relationship. Otherwise his inquiry into the nature and structure of the world would conjure up a world-picture in which man finds no place at all. He would remain an eccentric manipulator of the world, like an outsider in the world-picture conjured up by modern science.

But the indisputable fact is that man is an integral part of the world in which he finds his being. Consequently, the central point of inquiry has to be the nature of man–world relationship within the framework of the world as a whole. It is this man–world relationship that forms the subject-matter of Yoga Darsana.

Yoga looks at the man–world relationship as it actually exists between the 'seer' and the 'seen'. It is a relationship born of interaction that constantly goes on between the two. Man is both the 'seer' and the 'seen' at one and the same time. He is a 'seer' through his psychosomatic organism, which is a product of cosmic evolution (*prakrtyapura*). Therefore, it is basic to the inquiry that man first clearly comprehends the complex, that is the man–world relationship which he reflects within his own being. 'Man is cosmic evolution become aware of itself.' Yoga, therefore, deals with 'awareness' which it describes as 'pure seeing.' Seeing distorted or blurred by any kind of identification is seeing gone wrong. This wrong seeing is described by Yoga as 'seeing through past experiences' and through words which enshrine experiences. Therefore, says Yoga, craving or appetite for experiences and words must cease for 'pure seeing' or free perception to emerge. And this is the essence of what has been stated in Sutras 12 to 16.

The following Sutras deal with *Samadhi*, which is the flowering of the 'seed' (*bija*) planted in man's being by *vrtti-nirodha*.

4
Towards Samadhi

SUTRAS 17 TO 22

17. *Vitarka-vicārānandāsmitātūpānugamāt Saṁprajñātah*
Vrtti-nirodha moving forward in association with logical reasoning brings about one kind of *Samadhi*; moving forward in association with investigative intelligence it brings about another kind of *Samadhi*; moving forward in association with a sense of blissfulness it brings about a third kind of *Samadhi*; and moving forward in association with a sense of 'I-am-ness' it brings about the fourth kind of *Samadhi*. All these four kinds of *Samadhi* are known as *Samprajnata* [knowledge- or wisdom-oriented] *Samadhi*.

18. *Virāmapratyayābhyāsapūrvah Saṁskāraśeṣo-nyah*
A qualitatively different kind of *Samadhi* comes into being as a result of an experiencing of a state of cessation or discontinuance preceded by *abhyasa* and the ending of *samskaras* [past impregnations].

19. *Bhavpratyayo videhaprakṛti-layānām*
The experience of bodiless beings moving with the flux of the phenomenal world ends up in a kind of *Samadhi* when these bodiless entities are dissolved in the deluge.

20. *Śraddhāvīryasmṛtisạmādhiprjñāpūrvaka itareṣām*
Other beings [with bodies] attain a kind of *Samadhi* through faith, energy, recollectedness and *Samadhi*-oriented intelligence.

21. *Tīvrasaṁvegānāmāsannah*
For those with intensified impulse it [*Samadhi*] is close.

22. *Mṛdumadhyādhimātratvāttato-pi viśeṣah*
It is closer still for those who are sensitive enough to see and distinguish the low, medium and high levels of intensity.

NOTES AND COMMENTS

The Yoga Sutras speak of two streams of consciousness. The one, the superficial or peripheral, is a stream of consciousness (*citta-nadi*) which is propelled by *vrttisarupya* (identification with the ideational choice-making movement). This is a conditioned stream of consciousness (*samsara-pragbhara*) burdened with past impregnations (*samskar*), and incapable of discriminating intelligence (*a-viveka-visaya-nimna*). This inevitably and repeatedly ends up in sin and sorrow (*papa-vaha*). Here 'sin' means only a failure to see 'what is' from moment to moment. This failure inevitably lands man in unending sorrow or sin (see the commentary of Vyasa).

Man, however, does not want sorrow. Confronted by it he seeks same easy escapes from it. But there is no easy escape from sin and sorrow. The only way open to man is to face it and see what happens. Facing it means looking at it without moving away from it, without indulging in choices which conjure up an ideational escape from the existential. This is a critical moment which life presents to man in the form of sorrow. Sorrow or pain is, naturally, a threat to survival. To meet this threat with conditioned consciousness is to invite more and more sorrow, because it was originally conditioned consciousness that had landed man in the sorrow from which now he seeks to escape. Consequently, the way he may escape or be free from it is to question the nature and structure of consciousness which repeatedly lands him in sorrow. To question this conditioned and conditioning consciousness is to cease indulging in ideational choice-making. And to opt freely for 'not-choosing' is to embark on a voyage of *vrtti-nirodha* or Yoga.

This voyage of Yoga is a voyage on the very waters of life. It is this voyage which is described in the Yoga Sutras as 'a freedom-oriented stream of awareness (*kaivalya pragbhara citta-nadi*). When, as a result of freely opting for not-choosing, one moves and lives with what is, one sees clearly the distinction between what conditions the mind and makes it revolve round and round in the vicious circle of conditioning, on the one hand, and on the other, what frees the mind from the death-grip of conditioning. This perception is the mother of discriminating intelligence (*viveka*). From now onwards, it is a movement of mind in freedom, associated with this discriminating intelligence (*kaivalya pragbhara viveka-visaya-nimna citta-nadi*). And it is this stream of awareness which leads man from blessedness to blessedness (*kalyana*), to the abiding good of man and of the world in which he lives.

It is in the light of this distinction between the two qualitatively different streams of consciousness (*citta-nadi*) that the Sutras, now under discussion, have to be understood.

Moving in freedom (*kaivalya*) and in the light of discriminating intelligence (*viveka*), man first moves in association with *vitarka*, (logical reasoning) of a special kind or quality. *Tarka* is inferential reasoning ending up in a static conclusion. But one now moves in association with a special and qualitatively different kind of logical reasoning. One looks at what is, within and without, and subjects it to the test of logical reasoning. This critical approach negates everything that is irrelevant to what actually is, and moves along with what is relevant to existence as a whole. It is this movement that ripens into *savitarka Samadhi*. That is, the underground 'seed' (*bija*) of *vrtti-nirodha* shooting up into a visible sapling, full of new life.

Logical reasoning has its own limitations and frontiers, but freedom knows no frontiers. The new sapling of life, born of a special kind of logical reasoning, must grow into a tree. It is this inner aspiration born of freedom that transcends *savitarka Samadhi* and launches one on a further voyage of Yoga. Now one moves, not in association with *vitarka*, but in association with *vicara*, which is investigative intelligence. It is a free inquiry into what is, an endless exploration into the very essence of life and being. This movement flowers into *savicara Samadhi*. And this very movement, carried over forward, along with the movement of existence as a whole, ripens into a sense of blissfulness (*ananda*), which is *Sananda Samadhi*.

And again, this *Sananda Samadhi* further ripens into a 'sense of pure I-am-ness' (*asmita*), devoid of all tensions, which generally are associated with the tension-ridden ego, as stated in II-6.

All these four kinds of *Samadhi* belong to a qualified view of existence as a whole. It is qualified because it needs something, some support, something to hold on to, in order to keep pace with the subtle movement of existential reality. It is like holding on to this or that log of wood with a view to floating on a fast-moving current. Hence all these four kinds of *Samadhi* are grouped under one head – *Samprajnata*. *Prajna* is intelligence. With the prefix *sam* it means right intelligence. And *prajnata* means that which is well understood and absorbed. *Samprajnata* thus means '*Samadhi* associated with right intelligence, flowering into wisdom'. Since this

Samadhi depends on such association it is a qualified *Samadhi*. A common thread of 'I-based' intelligence runs through all these four kinds of *Samadhi*. It begins with I-based logical reasoning and ends up in a sense of pure 'I-am-ness'. This pure 'I-am-ness' is devoid of any attribute and hence clean and self-radiant. Like a 'point', it has position but no magnitude of any kind, material or mental. It just declares that 'I am I; I am not the other, and never can be the other'. It is existential aloneness, full of the energy of being, not wanting to become anything else, because it sees clearly that any movement towards 'becoming' is a movement away from 'being' and therefore, a self-alienating movement. It thus lives peacefully and with a sense of bliss with what is, within and without. All its activities are charged with this existential sense of aloneness which never reacts to anything with any tinge of hostility. It has nothing to lose and, perhaps, a whole world to gain.

While this is existential wisdom, it lacks one thing – the unfolding of the mystery underlying the man–world relationship. The sense of pure 'I-am-ness' and aloneness is still experiencing the world, but is unable to make sense out of it. That is to say, it is still experience-oriented and not pure seeing-oriented. It is still *pratyayanu-pasyata* and not *suddha drsimatrata* (II-20).

Something has to happen to end this experience-oriented sense of being, because experience is knowledge-based, and to know is to become the known. Although one in *Sasmita Samadhi* lives from moment to moment, that is, from experience to experience without leaning on the past, he still remains an 'I-based' entity, with 'I' as the experiencer and the world as an object of experiencing.

Seeing this situation, and seeing the limitation in this duality-based, qualified way of living and being, one is always on the lookout for some explosion from within. It is this explosion about which Sutra 18 speaks.

It speaks of '*virma-pratya*', i.e. the experiencing of cessation or discontinuance. This is born of *abhyasa*, the empty interval devoid of any *vrtti*, i.e. experience. It is experiencing a break in the continuity or succession of experiences, one after the other, endlessly. It is not an experience of any 'thing'; it is actually cessation of experiencing with 'I' at the centre. This is the beginning of 'pure seeing' with no centre. With 'I' as the operating centre gone away, it is like experiencing and seeing without either the experiencer or the 'seer' as a fixed point of reference. Because there is no centre or a fixed point, around which alone experiences can gather and weave a web of *samskaras* (impregnations of experiences), the old *samskaras* wither away. They wither away because there is no point of fixity around which alone they can gather and weave a pattern of conditioning, in which unwary and unaware men get imprisoned.

This is an altogether new and qualitatively different state of being and is later called *nirvitarka, nirvicara, nirbija Samadhi.* This extraordinary state of being is complete in itself, embracing the totality of existence. It is no longer in need of any support in the form of logical reasoning, investigative intelligence, blissfulness or pure I-am-ness. It is all-inclusive and yet eternally free from holding on to anything as an anchorage. It is like the totality that is man, in perfect harmony with the mystery underlying man-world relationship.

Sutras 19 and 20 speak of those who have not, or would not, opt for *vrtti-nirodha.* These fall under two types of beings: the bodiless, and those with bodies. Those who die and thus become bodiless entities will continue to move in a stream of consciousness that remains ever associated with the flux in which the world moves. And since it is a permanent property of mind (*citta-dharma*) to attain *Samadhi*, sooner or later, these bodiless beings will attain *Samadhi* at the time of the final deluge. This is rather an intriguing statement. We must leave it alone; leave it to perfect Yogis to explain, if and when they may choose to do so.

The other type of men are those who are still living with bodies, but who do not or will not opt for not-choosing. For the benefit of these men a four-fold way is suggested. These are men who must have something to believe in. Sutra 20 suggests to these men that if they must believe then let them put implicit trust and faith (*sraddha*) in the discipline of Yoga. If one lives with intensity in such faith in Yoga, then this faith itself will generate an upsurge of new energy. This energy, in its turn, will bring about a state of recollectedness a state in which one can look at the whole structure of impregnations which constitute conditioned consciousness, at a glance. Lastly, this faith–energy–recollectedness combination will burst forth into a *Samadhi*-oriented intelligence. In this manner, this four-fold way will flower into *Samadhi.*

Sutras 21 and 22 emphasize the necessity of having high intensity and a very subtle and delicate sensitivity as necessary requirements for *Samadhi.* Psychosomatic intensity, attentive sensitivity and intelligence merge together and explode into a mutational transformation. *Samadhi* is a name given to such transformation.

The remaining Sutras of this Part I deal with a few alternative ways to *vrtti-nirodha* and *Samadhi*. They end in a brief exposition of '*Seedless Samadhi*' – the Omega or apex of Yoga discipline.

5
The Way of God-awareness

SUTRAS 23 TO 29

23. *Īṣvarapraṇidhānātvā*
Or [alternatively] through reverential God-awareness.
24. *Kleśakarmavipākāśayairāparamṛṣṭah puruṣaviśeṣah Īṣvarah*
One remaining untouched by tension, tension-born action, action-born fruit and fruit-born accumulation–which all together form the conditioned psyche–becomes *Purusa* in a special sense. This special in man is God.
25. *Tatra niratiśayaṁ sārvajña bījaṁ*
There [in God] abides the seed of all-knowingness.
26. *Sa eṣah pūrveṣāmapi guruh kalenānavacchedāt*
He alone is the Guru of all by-gone gurus, because unbound by time.
27. *Tasya vācakah praṇavah*
He is signified by *pranava*, i.e. OM.
28. *Tajjapastadartha-bhāvanam*
Constant awareness of what is signified by OM is called *japa* [slow inward, attentive muttering of OM].
29. *Tatah pratyakcetanādhigamo-pyaṅtarāyābhāvaśca*
Thereby comes about an inward understanding and the negation of all impediments [to God-awareness and *Samadhi*].

NOTES AND COMMENTS

From this Sutra up to Sutra 39, seven ways alternative to *abhyasa-vairagya* (Sutra 12) are suggested for bringing about *citta-vrtti-nirodha*, which flowers into *Samadhi*. Just as for those who do not, or would not, opt for not-choosing, the way of faith (Sutra 20) is suggested, so also these seven alternatives are suggested for all who come across unforeseen impediments to remaining undisturbed in the state of *nirodha* (i.e. a state of mind devoid of any *vrtti*). Out of these seven alternatives, the present group of Sutras deals with the alternative named as 'reverential God-God-awareness' —*isvarapranidhana*.

Just as *biologically* two basic urges, self-preservation and self-procreation, dominate human life on the physiological level, so also *psychologically* two basic tendencies (*vrttis*) seem to dominate human life on the cultural level. One is a sense of wonder; and the other is a sense of worship. The sense of wonder gives rise to a spirit of free inquiry which brings into being sciences, arts, literature and philosophy, which all together weave a certain pattern of culture. On the other hand, the sense of worship is generally accompanied by a feeling of total surrender to that 'mysterious something' which lies beyond human comprehension. This 'mysterious and awe-inspiring something' is signified by the word 'God'. Such a sense of worship and total surrender to 'God' constitutes a religious feeling, around which organized religions are established. It also brings about mystic experiences which, strangely enough, appear to be similar irrespective of times, places, races and circumstances.

It could therefore be maintained, tentatively and not dogmatically, that whereas the sense of wonder is more intellectual than emotional, the sense of worship is more emotional than intellectual. Two cannot be separated, but they are clearly distinguishable. The two together make up the psychic energy of a human being, and the assumed dichotomy between the two results in a variety of split personalities (or forms of schizophrenia).

The approach of Yoga to human life is *integral* as opposed to *analytical*. The latter approach inevitably divides man, within and without.

The way of God-awareness, which these Sutras expound, cuts across all concepts about God prevalent either in the East or in the West. The conceptual approach is basically ideational as opposed to existential or real. Not warring concepts, ideas, ideologies and systematized thought-patterns or theories – theocratic or secular – but *man*, the maker of all these dream-like patterns, is the subject-matter of Yoga. Therefore, existentially, God cannot be anything over and above man, or other than man. *He* has to be 'something' within the very being of man, of which, because of the thick layers of conditioning accumulated from time immemorial, man remains unaware. These Sutras are primarily intended to enable man to be vitally and intensely aware of that 'something' of very special quality that vibrates within him, which is vaguely named 'God'.

Man, as a phenomenon, is obviously a complex of conditionings – evolutionary and socio-cultural. At the same time, man carries within his psyche two basic tendencies – the sense of wonder and the sense of worship. Both bring about some kind of a transcendence of evolutionary and socio-cultural complexes. These complexes are described in Sutra 24 as being the products of four basic factors: tensions; tension-born activities; activity-born fruits; and fruit-born accumulations in the psyche, which together prevent man from a right comprehension of his existential identity. By opting for not-choosing it is possible for man to remain untouched by any or all of these four factors. But if one finds it difficult to opt for *vrtti-nirodha* then he should at least take a firm stand on that 'Great Unknown' which inheres in his being and which he calls 'God'.

God, the Great Unknown, must ever remain undefinable, because that which is timeless cannot be defined. All definitions are temporal and mental constructs, which must cease for the timeless to be. What is stated in Sutra 24 is not therefore a definition of God. It only draws man's attention to the necessity of negating the four factors which together constitute his conditioned consciousness. One cannot remain caught up in tensions, tension-born activities, activity-born fruits and fruit-born accumulations which together dominate his psyche, and still hope to establish any meaningful relationship with God. Only the negation of these four basic factors will enable man to be aware of his existential identity. It is this very special kind of self-awareness which will bring man face to face with that which is named as God. It would then be like man looking in a mysterious mirror which does not reflect back the face of man but the face of that 'mysterious something' which man has been calling by the name 'God'.

Sutra 25 states that this 'vision' of God carries within it the seed of all-knowingness. Whatever man is able to know is actually a mere fragment, a partial experience of the phenomenal world. Man's very capacity to know has its source in something everlastingly mysterious and incomprehensible. Knowledge is the creation of man's mind. But that mysterious something which enables man to know at all, is not, and can never be, man's creation. Even the mind of man is not man's creation. The mind-generated ideational choice-making movement produces what man calls 'knowledge'. This knowledge is always of the past. It is not experiencing here and now, but the product of accumulated experiences of past and bygone events. These accumulations (*asaya*), founded on past impregnations, trigger the movement of fragmentary knowing, which is basically ideational. What man calls 'knowledge' is therefore, not only fragmentary but devoid of direct *experiencing* of the real or the existential. Man's entanglement in the prison-house of such knowledge must end for real experiencing and knowing to be. And this becomes possible only when man becomes capable of remaining untouched and uninfluenced by the operation of the four factors mentioned in Sutra 24. The negation or elimination of these four factors that dominate man's psychical and cultural life places man in direct touch with the source of 'all-knowingness'.

Sutra 26 states that this primeval source of all-knowingness, this God, is the real Guru of all gurus that appear in human forms from time to time. Guru, the God, is not time-bound. 'He' is 'timeless something' – the source of cosmic energy, that brings enlightenment to man's being only if he takes care to remain untouched by the operation of the four factors that condition and dominate his day-to-day life. It is always there, and remain unaffected by time, place or circumstance.

The word *Guruh* technically means 'one who performs the purificatory ceremonies over a boy and instructs him in the Vedas,' i.e. the 'sacred knowledge'. In esoteric terms this purificatory ceremony means 'initiation' whereby the slumbering energy of 'seeing awareness' is awakened in the disciple. 'Initiation' does not mean imparting knowledge in the ordinary sense. It means purification (*suddhi*) of mind and liberation from the accumulated rubbish called knowledge, which creates impediments to the perception of truth or reality. The removal of this rubbish is 'purification', or '*suddhi*' – a word which the Yoga Sutras use in many places. The plethora of 'gurus' that is found rampant all over the world today, and has been more or less so from time immemorial is a monstrous distortion of the word 'Guru' as used in these Sutras.

Since these Sutras equate 'God' with 'Guru', and since this 'Guru' has no material or mental form, and again, since man needs to hold this formless something in his awareness to be able to 'see' God or perceive reality, Sutra 27 states that '*Pranava*' or 'OM' is the word which signifies 'God' or 'Guru'. The word *Pranava* is derived from the word *nava* with the prefix *pra*. It means 'ever fresh, ever new'. (*Prakarsena nava-navah, navanavonmesah = Pranavah*). Ever fresh and ever new flashes of enlightenment is *Pranava* or OM, the worldless word, which is equated with the negation of the four factors mentioned in Sutra 24. Constant awareness of this is real *japa*. It is not a mechanical repetition of any word, including OM. OM is just an aid to awakening slumbering awareness. It has to be a word-like sound, since man and word are correlated, they imply and necessitate each other – man being a 'language animal'.

Sutra 29 states that this aid to maintaining constant awareness of God, of itself brings understanding and negates all mind-made impediments to *citta-vrtti-nirodha* and the consequent state of choiceless awareness, which is *Samadhi*.

The following few Sutras give a precise exposition of these mind-made impediments, so that one becomes clearly aware of the mischief they do in the matter of destroying or distorting the discipline of Yoga.

6
Impediments on the Way

SUTRAS 30 TO 33

30. *Vyādhi-styāna-saṅśaya-pramādā-lasyā-virati-bhrāntidarśanā-labdhabhūmikatvā-navasthitatvāni cittavikṣepāste-aṅtarāvāh*

Sickness, inertia, doubt, mistake, idleness, greed, illusory visions, a sense of failure in reaching the foothold of Yoga, non-establishment on the path of Yoga, even after having touched it for a time– these nine are the distortions and dissipations of mind, called 'antarāya' or impediments [which one comes across] on the way to Yoga.

31. *Dukkha, dourmanasyā-ṅgamejayatva, ṣvāsapraṣvāsa vikṣepa-sahabhuvah*

Pain or sorrow, irritation caused by non-fulfilment of desire, trembling of the body, unnatural incoming and outgoing of the breath, these four distortions accompany the scattered mind.

32. *Tatpratiṣedhārtham-ekatatvābhyāsah*

For the warding off of these impediments one-pointed *abhyasa* is suggested.

33. *Maitrī-karuṇā-mudito-pekṣānām sukha-dukkha-puṇyāpuṇya visayānām bhāvanā taṣcitta prasādanaṁ*

Friendliness, compassion, joyousness and indifference, in respect of the objects of happiness, sorrow, virtue and non-virtue lead to purity and clarity of mind.

NOTES AND COMMENTS

A careful look at this detailed recording of impediments one comes across while on way to Yoga, will show that the nine impediments mentioned in Sutra 30 are actually nine forms of *vrttis* that arise one after the other when one sees the necessity of opting for not making choices. Opting for not making choices is itself a *vrtti.* But it is of a kind that cuts across the very roots of ideational choice-making. It is an exercise of freedom in the form of a negative action. Or, it is like swimming against the current of *vrttisarypya* (identifications). This counter-movement towards the very source of the choice-making tendency is bound to disturb the whole complex of the conditioned psyche. It is a clash between two different kinds of energy – the downward moving energy of conditioning, like the downward pull of gravitation, on the one hand, and the upward moving energy accompanying the vision of the necessity of not-choosing in the interests of freedom and liberation from entanglement with *vrttisarupya* or the current of conditioning, on the other. The very first impediment one encounters on this strange voyage of Yoga is a feeling of sickness (*vyadhi*). This is not a sickness with which we are familiar in our conditioned day-to-day living. It is an altogether different kind of sickness. It is in a sense of revolt against the habit-forming tendency, which, in fact, is an ever-persisting psychosomatic ailment or disease, but which we mistakenly equate with health and wellbeing. To be taken over by any habit is to deaden sensitivity to 'what is'. And it is this that is rudely shaken by the very first step towards Yoga and it results in this strange kind of sickness.

The second impediment one comes across is a sense of inertia (*styana*). This again is an inertia on an entirely different level. One comes upon it as a result of overcoming the first impediment, followed by a sense of some exhaustion consequent on fighting it out. It is inertia in the reverse order. Natural or conditioned inertia is always at the mercy of forces external to it. This new sense of inertia (*styana*) is the outcome of a temporary exhaustion consequent on the upward march of a totally self-reliant inner energy.

The third impediment is *sansaya* – a doubt, a temporary inability to distinguish between the old and the new inertia. While in this state of doubt, that is, of being in two minds, one is apt to feel mistaken, that is, mistaken about the rightness of the way of Yoga one has opted for. This mistake-making (*pramada*) is the fourth impediment. But this cannot last long because the moment one becomes aware of the absolute rightness of not-choosing, the mistake-making propensity vanishes from view. One is thus back again on the path of Yoga. But this coming back on the path of Yoga generates another impediment. It is the sense of assurance that one will not hereafter commit any more mistakes. This feeling of assurance is a *vrtti* which makes one deviate from the path by inducing one to become idle (*alasya*). This is a kind of heaviness of mind and body. This leads to another impediment, namely *avirati* or greed for the objects of the senses. But seeing the horror of this greed, as being a throwback to the past, one comes out of it only to fall into another trap. It is now not objects of the physical senses, but objects of extra-sensory perception. *Alasya* (idleness) is like a psychic sleep in which one tends to dream. So one sees visions of gods or gurus, or of something so strange that one tends to attribute the phenomenon to a 'divine visitation'. Much is generally made of such strange visions, as though they indicate some higher level of being and experiencing. As a matter of fact these visions (*bhranti-darsana*) belong to the stuff of which any ordinary dreams are made. Dreams are of two kinds: those that are physiologically induced and those that are psychologically induced. In either case they are a variety of the *vrtti* named previously *viparyaya* (I-6). Yoga, therefore, rejects these so-called 'divine visitations' as wholly illusory.

When one gets over the impediments of *alasya, avirati* and *bhrantidarsan* (5, 6 and 7), one is confronted with another impediment, called *alabdha-bhumi-katva*, i.e. a sense of failure in feeling that one has not been able so far to even touch the firm ground of Yoga. This impediment, the eighth, is an outcome of a sense of failure despite the energetic interest taken in Yoga and the effort made in that direction so far. But this sense of failure cannot last long because one sees that there is now no going back to the old horror of *vrttisarupya* (conditioned consciousness and the misery it inevitably entails). Seeing this with clarity automatically liquidates the sense of failure; and one then tends to make peace with 'what is', whatever it may be. This leads suddenly to an actual touching of the ground of Yoga. And one is then naturally overjoyed. But this is an unbalanced sense of accomplishment – a *vrtti* which negates one's touch of the ground of Yoga, even though one really had it. This lands one in the ninth and the last impediment, called '*anavasthitatva*', non-establishment of oneself on the firm ground of being, i.e. Yoga, despite having actually touched it for a time. Here again one sees the error of being impatient – the most powerfully seductive trick of temporality. Temporality or identification with the unending sequences of past–present–future, is the last and the most powerful impediment to establishment in *Yoga-bhumika*. At this point one has to see that it is the time-temporal sequence – which is at the very root of all other kinds of conditionings. It is time or temporality that lies at the bottom of the unending sequences of hope–despair–hope–despair . . . It is identification with this mind-made stratagem that is most difficult to circumvent. This impediment could be overcome only if one takes a good look at impatience to which one succumbs repeatedly. What is impatience? Is it not a desire to achieve, to attain, to accomplish, to succeed quickly in our goal? But is Yoga a goal capable of being reached by any egocentric effort? Has one not already seen that the first step towards Yoga is to opt freely for not-choosing, wherever it may lead? And having taken this step, where is the goal, a utopia born of this or that *vrtti*? And what relevance has impatience to this altogether new adventure – a voyage on the waters of the Great Unknown?

It is this kind of questioning and meditation that eliminates the seductive power of temporality, working through the *vrtti* of impatience. One then sees the truth, that remaining in a state of choiceless awareness with alert attention toward each and every *vrtti* that rises up, stays for a while and then disappears, is the one and only way to keep one's feet firmly on the ground of existential reality. Choiceless awareness, from moment to moment is the master key capable of opening any door that operates as an impediment on the path of Yoga. It is a path which has nothing to do with either time or space that dominates the external world. It is a path in a world of an altogether totally new dimension, or rather a world to which no verbal description can ever apply. Words, experiences and temporality must cease for the world of Yoga to be.

Sutra 31 speaks of collateral disturbances that generally accompany the nine impediments enumerated in the last Sutra. These are named as pain or sorrow (*dukkha*), irritation caused by non-fulfilment of any desire (*daurmanasya*), trembling of the body (*angamejavatva*), and unnatural or troublesome incoming and outgoing of the breath. The point to be noted in connection with these four collateral disturbances is that once you opt for the way of Yoga you are in for all kinds of troubles caused by the resistance which a mind conditioned by *vrttisurupya* must necessarily offer to *vrtti-nirodha* in which it sees its death. The whole complex of the psychosomatic organization is violently shaken to its very foundations by the negative act of choicelessness and living with the state of non-identification with *vrttis*. It is a beginning of a mutational transformation in the entire realm of conditioned consciousness. Consequently, one who has opted for Yoga must necessarily be prepared for all kinds of storms and foul weather occasioned by the operation of last-ditch battles of resistance from the conditioned consciousness. The body and the psyche, once they have been drawn out from their citadel of safety, comfort and security, must do everything in their power to dissuade one from going ahead on the path of Yoga. Sutras 30 and 31 describe what forms this resistance to change takes in one's body and mind.

Sutra 32 suggests one-pointed adherence to *abhyasa*, i.e. to stay firm in a void devoid of *vrttis*. This void will repeatedly be filled and disturbed violently by storms of *vrttis* pushed up to the surface by the power of the past-propelled momentum. All such storms will appear, cause troubles, and disappear by themselves because one has ceased to get identified with them. The pushing force having thus ceased to operate, the momentum of the wheels of *vrttis* must necessarily slow down and come to a halt. It needs tremendous energy of quietude that naturally accompanies clarity of perception. It is the clouding of perception that creates all the difficulties. Therefore, one-pointed adherence to *abhyasa* is suggested to ward off all difficulties '*eka-tattva*' in Sutra 32, appearing as an attribute of *abhyasa*, is not any ideal, or ideational principle apart from *abhyasa*, as defined in Sutra 13. Energetic interest in *sthiti*, or a state of void devoid of *vrttis*, (which is *abhyasa*), is itself potent enough to ward off and overcome all possible impediments to Yoga.

The compound *eka-tatva-abhyasa* means *abhyasa* as the one and only sovereign, all-inclusive principle of life. *Tat-tva* means 'thatness'. 'Thatness' of everything is what actually pervades the whole world, including one's psychosomatic organism. 'It' is not mine or yours. No one can claim 'it' as one's exclusive property. Therefore, a state of void, devoid of *vrttis* (*abhyasa*), on the one hand, and 'thatness' of everything, on the other, is precondition of being in a state, called Yoga – a state of rapport with existence as a whole. This is what is signified by *eka-tat tvabhyasa*.

Sutra 33 comes after all impediments are warded off by the reinforcement of *abhyasa*, as suggested in the previous Sutra. The waters of the mind are now clear and calm after the waves of many storms have disappeared. There is now nothing that disturbs the calm waters of the mind. And just as the still waters of a lake reflect clearly the skies above, so also the still waters of the mind now reflect clearly the reality that is life. This reality generates four feelings which perform the role of keeping the waters of the mind clear and pure for all time. Temporality cannot touch the stillness of these waters because these feelings are the creations of stillness itself. The disturbances hereafter will come from two dichotomies, each different from the other. One is the dichotomy between pleasure and pain, or happiness and unhappiness. The other is the dichotomy between virtue and non-virtue. Pleasure and pain are the two basic forms which human experiences take. These have nothing to do with right and wrong, true and false, good and bad. They are inherent qualities (*dharmas*) of experiences. And it is only after the repeated sequences of these pleasure-pain oriented experiences are impregnated on the brain cells or the mind-stuff, and as a result of this man is faced with misery they entail, that man invents some ethical standards to ward off the misery. Virtue and non-virtue now come on the scene of human life. But the avoidance of non-virtue or sin, and adherence to virtue or non-sin, are incapable of resolving the misery that the dichotomy between pain and pleasure generates. One cannot end one dichotomy by another dichotomy. Dichotomy itself must cease for life to move on in freedom and creativity.

Sutra 33 suggests exactly this way of resolving all threats to purity and clarity of mind which came in the form of these two basic dichotomies. When the mind is still and crystal clear it generates a feeling of friendliness that knows no frontiers. It embraces the whole world, human and non-human. No tension, conflict or duality can touch it. It is sovereign in its existential authenticity.

It is this feeling (*bhavana*) of friendliness (*maitri*) which imparts such a delicate sensitivity to the mind that it melts into a feeling of compassion (*karuna*) whenever it looks at misery or pain in any being. It declares to humanity as a whole, in its language of sacred silence, that the only way to banish misery from life is to be friendly and compassionate to all beings. And the very perception of this truth brings a feeling of such a joy (*mudita*) to the mind that it will never even dream of doing anything inconsistent with the discipline of Yoga.

Meditation (*bhavanatah*) on this trinity of feelings keeps the mind pure and crystal clear so that perception of truth or reality is never clouded. One whose mind has thus attained such purity and clarity remains in a state of *upeksa*, from moment to moment. This word is derived from the root *iksa*, which means 'to see'. With the prefix *upa*, which means 'nearness, contiguity', *upeksa* would mean 'to be, or to remain in a state of nearness to the energy of pure seeing', without expecting (*apeksa*) anything. In this state of meditation the entire energy of one's being converges on 'seeing', to the total exclusion of all *vrttis*.

In the following few Sutras alternative ways to *citta-vrtti-nirodha*, besides the way of God-awareness, are expounded. We shall deal with them in the next chapter.

7
The Alternative Ways

SUTRAS 34 TO 39

34. *Pracchardana-vidhāraṇābhvāṁvā prāṇasya*
Alternatively, meditation on holding the breath in after inhalation and out after exhalation also brings about *citta-vritti-nirodha.*

35. *Viṣayavatī va pravṛttirutpannā-manasah sthitinibaṅdhinī*
Or meditation on the arising of an intensified interest in association with any object holds the mind in a steady state.

36. *Viśokā vā jyotiṣmatī*
Or meditation on the arising of an intensified interest in a state devoid of grief, and having the quality of illumination, also holds the mind in a steady state.

37. *Vitarāgaviṣayaṁ vā cittaṁ*
Or meditation on that state of mind which remains uncoloured or unaffected by any object, also brings about a state of quietude to the mind.

38. *Svapna-nidrā-jñānālaṁbanaṁvā*
Or meditation on the experience or knowledge gained in sleep or in a dream, also brings about a state of quietude to the mind.

39. *Yathābhimata-dhyānādvā*
Or meditation on a subject in which one is naturally interested also brings about a state of quietude to the mind.

NOTES AND COMMENTS

As has already been stated, from Sutras 23 to 39, ways alternative to *abhyasa* and *vairagya* are suggested, which help one embrace the discipline of Yoga. What distinguishes these alternative ways from the primary way of *abhyasa-vairagya* is that whereas in the latter there is total rejection of words and experiences leading to a steady state (*sthiti*) devoid of *vrttis*, in the former there is dependence on one intensified interest to the total rejection of all fragmentary *vrttis*. Therefore, whereas *abhyasa-vairagya* leads first to a qualified *Samadhi* and thereafter to an unqualified *Samadhi*, these alternative ways lead only to a steady state of mind (*sthiti*) in which the necessity and supreme importance of *abhyasa-vairagya* becomes crystal clear for one's firm establishment in the discipline of Yoga.

It is necessary to appreciate the distinction between the primary and the secondary ways. The basic question that arises in relation to the Yogic way of life and the non-Yogic way is: what is the nature and significance of man's relationship to the world in which he finds his being? What is it that relates man to the outside world, which ordinarily makes no sense to him, or which remains a perpetual question-mark before his eyes? He may utilize the objective world for his ends; he may discover tools for a better and more efficacious exploitation of the external world for his own egocentric ends; and he may entertain a feeling of hope or certainty that the discovery of more effective tools is the only way open to man to establish his mastery over the entire order of the world of nature.

But despite more than two million years of man's existence on this wonderful earth, and over three hundred years of breath-taking discoveries in the field of science and technology, the basic question of the nature and significance of man's relationship with man and nature still remains a big question-mark. In fact, it has never been raised and looked into with any seriousness at all. The only people who raised it and pursued it to the bitter end were the Vedic and Buddhist seers. And it is the perceptions of these seers and their far-reaching and almost devastating implications, that forms the subject matter of Yoga Darsana.

This question is specifically dealt with in Part IV of the text. Sutras 16 and 17 of this Part state that *vastu*, or reality, is not of such a nature that it can be manipulated at will by any individualized mind. And mind is all that man has that may enable him to discover the existential nature and realistic significance of his relationship with the external world, human and non-human. The objective world, in which man finds his being, is there in its own majesty and sovereignty. It exists and persists – irrespective of man's existence or otherwise on this planet. The question is: what is it that brings man's mind into a meaningful relationship with *vastu* or the objective world? The answer is: man's passionate interest in *vastu* or the objective world.

Man must go to natural sources of waters when he feels thirsty. He must find food in the natural world when he feels hungry. This is an existential imperative. There can be no escape from it unless man wants to commit suicide. And, if he opts for this fatal alternative, which, of course, is open to him because of the freedom with which he is born, then the whole game is over. Therefore the passionate interest in *vastu* or the objective world which is integrally associated with his survival, furnishes the only significant link (Yoga) between man and the world. And exploration into the nature and significance of this natural link may alone reveal the *raison d'ētre* of man's existence on this earth and in this vast and unbounded universe. In the absence of an intense interest in this basic inquiry, all other inquiries unrelated to it must necessarily end in one or other kind of delusion.

Yoga, therefore, maintains that, since the nature-given passionate interest in *vastu* is a must for the very survival of man, it is this that must form the basic subject-matter of man's inquiry, with a view to discovering the nature and significance of man's relationship with the world. It is this passionate interest in *vastu* on which depends man's act of experiencing and knowing anything. In the absence of such existentially ordained passionate interest, there would be no experiencing and no knowing of anything whatsoever. The world as *vastu* must remain knowable or unknowable, depending upon man's passionate interest, or lack of interest, in *vastu*.

It should now be clear why Yoga draws man's attention to the supreme necessity of a purity and clarity of vision (*darsana*) for understanding the nature and significance of his relationship with the objective word, and, secondly, why Yoga draws man's attention to the other correlated basic fact that such purity and clarity of vision would be possible only if man's mind is freed from all blind, self-deluding and self-destroying identifications with his *vrttis*.

The Sutras therefore, lay down that there are two ways of bringing the mind to that steady state (*sthiti*) in which alone perception of what is, within and without, in its existential authenticity, is possible: (i) opting freely, effortlessly for not-choosing, which naturally leads to *abhyasa* and *vairagya*; and (ii) meditation on any kind of passionate interest in any *vastu* or real object, to the exclusion of all fragmentary *vrttis*. It should be noted that the first and primary way is also based on a passionate interest in *vastu*; but it is interest without dependence on anything; whereas the second way is dependent on a passionate interest in one or the other real object. In either case it is passionate interest in *vastu* that links man to the objective world in an existential sense – as opposed to all manner of ideation or *vrttis*. There is a distinction between a passionate interest in *vastu*; and a *vrtti*. In the former it is the whole mind, the totality of it, that gets involved in passionate interest in *vastu*; whereas *vrtti* is a fragmentary upsurge in the mind-stuff triggered by built-in-likes or dislikes, or by some past impregnations on the brain cells or by one's mind getting activated by what one sees or experiences in the present.

It is this existentially ordained passionate interest in *vastu* (*taduparaga*) that forms the subject-matter of Yoga Darsana. And the Sutras tell us that an inquiry into the nature and significance of this passionate interest in *vastu* has to remain at a level in which identification with anything, mental or non-mental, has no place at all, because such identification is tantamount to an abdication of free and objective inquiry.

Sutra 34 furnishes a very telling example of the kind of inquiry Yoga has in view. This Sutra draws attention to the natural or existential phenomenon of breathing. Breathing and living are so intertwined that, broadly speaking, they are correlative, they imply and necessitate each other. If one is passionately interested in living, a time may come when breathing, a correlate of living, may excite one's equally passionate interest in it. This could not be just an idle or flippant *vrtti* of curiosity. It would demand total attention and involve the totality of one's mind, as much as passionate interest in living involves the totality of one's being. The moment this happens one begins to observe one's ever-going breathing with total and alert attention. This is what is meant by the word *dhyana* or meditation. It is not thinking, speculating or imagining. It is 'pure seeing', objective observation in which nothing subjective has any place. The first thing one discovers in a state of such meditation is that statements such as 'I breathe' or 'my breathing' are utterly baseless. Breathing goes on whether one makes or does not make any statement about it. It has nothing to do with man's irrepressible tendency to chatter about things. One is thus in a state in which utter silence reigns supreme. There is seeing, observing, perceiving. But even this has nothing to do with 'me' or 'mine'. Seeing, perceiving is as much a given fact as breathing. Seeing, perceiving makes one *aware* of the existential fact of breathing. That is all there is to it. It is not *my* awareness or *anybody else's* awareness. There is 'seeing' on the one hand, and 'breathing' on the other. The two are not one. They are two distinct things, both natural and existential. And what links them with each other is the arising of passionate interest in breathing as integrated with living. This passionate interest belongs to mind (*citta*) as a whole. The mind is now so fully involved in this passionate interest that there is no room in it for any fragmentary *vrtti*. It is the wholeness of mind, in a state of steady quietude that brings into being the discipline of Yoga. And it is this steady state of quietude that reflects the 'seer' (or 'pure seeing') on the one hand, and the 'seen' (in this case 'breathing' as a natural phenomenon), on the other. The two existential realities are brought together in an immensely meaningful relationship. Perception and objectivity are related to each other in pristine purity and beauty.

While in this state one makes wonderful discoveries. One notices that at the end of inhalation of the breath and at the end of its exhalation there is a slight pause, a halt which shatters the concept of continuity – which was the product of *vrtti-sarupya* in which one was entangled before this new and unique state of meditation. One now sees that nothing in this universe is continuous. At the bottom of apparent continuity there is a movement of discontinuity which is the very quality of life as a whole.

After this extraordinary perception one notices that the pauses at the end of inhalation and exhalation begin to lengthen and to impart to the steady state an extraordinary depth, which seems to embrace the whole mystery of relationship between life and the objective world. The original 'passionate interest' now acquires the illumination of intelligence. It is thus that one suddenly discovers the significance of a statement which comes later in Part II, to the effect that meditation on breathing eliminates the coverings on inner enlightenment (II-52). An astounding discovery! It is no longer an isolated act of breathing by an inconsequential individual. It is as though the air, that constitutes an integral part of the objective world, has a message to give. The breathing entity – that one stupidly names as the 'I' or the 'me' – is a significant focal point on which the whole objective world converges and offers an experience which merges into 'seeing' and, so to speak renews itself, giving a new richness and an ever new significance to it. It is as though there is a giving and a taking going on from moment to moment, in which neither time nor space nor circumstance seem relevant to experiencing and seeing. It is a vital, dynamic and meaningful ecological equilibrium between the 'seer' and the 'seen'. The reality of pure perception thus carries with it an ecological significance. The ecological imbalance now posing a threat to the survival of life on earth, in the form of global pollution, is thus actually seen as a product of perception gone wrong and mind gone mad.

One also makes the discovery that there is a vital connection between the pauses coming at the end of inhalation and exhalation and the *sthiti* or the steady state of quietude of the mind. Both furnish a firm foundation for the dynamic and creative discipline of Yoga.

Sutra 35 furnishes another equally telling example of how meditation on something of passionate interest, suddenly arising in the mind in respect of a real object, leads to a steady state of quietude which flowers into *Samadhi*. For instance, one falls in love with a person of the opposite sex. The passionate interest in the particular object – a person of the opposite sex – involves the totality of mind leaving no room for any fragmentary movement in the form of *vrttis*. Many stormy events will happen if the person – the object of intense passion – does not respond in the expected way. Even so, the passion reigns supreme over the entire mind, forcing meditation on its nature and its significance for one's life. This meditation leads to the discovery of the real, existential nature of the relationship between one human being and the other. Friendliness, compassion and the bliss of human relationship are thus unfolded to the view, removing all the dark layers of previous conditioning clouding one's perception. It is no longer the particular person that now dominates the scene, but 'passionate interest' that unfolds the mystery underlying human relationships as a whole; it leads to a momentous discovery that without love everything is an arid land in which not a blade of grass will ever grow. It is this that brings calm in which all the storms find their ultimate repose. The 'passionate interest' now flowers into a clarity and purity of vision which establishes one in the discipline of Yoga.

The remaining Sutras of the group under consideration have to be understood in the same way. It is not necessary to understand all these alternative ways. Any one of these that triggers one's passionate interest is enough for the purpose.

It should be obvious from the foregoing discussion that Yoga is not a dogmatic doctrine or a closed system of thought or ideology. On the contrary all such systematized thought processes are a hindrance to Yoga. All that Yoga demands from man is a passionate interest in anything which links him vitally to any real object (*vastu*). This is made absolutely clear in Sutra 39. 'Passionate interest' is essential because without it there can be no real basis for serious exploration into the existential nature of man's relationship with man and the objective world. Men who cannot bring themselves to take a passionate interest in any real object must unfortunately be written off as somewhat less than human. They will go on living like logs of dead wood tossed hither and thither by external winds on the waters of life.

8
From Steady State to Reflecting State

SUTRAS 40 TO 46

40. *Paramāṇuparamamahattvānto-sya vaśīkārah*

The sweep of the steady mind [*asya*] ranges from infinitely small particles to infinitely great skies.

41. *Kṣīṇavṛtterabhijātasyeva maṇergrahītṛgrahaṇagrāhejeṣn taṭsthatadañjanatā Samāpattih*

With the ending of the movement of choice-making tendency, the steady mind becomes stainless and pure like a crystal, reflecting the interaction between the receiver and the received which takes place through the senses. This quality of sensitive reflectivity is called *Samapatti*.

42. *Tatra śabdārthajñānavikalpaih saṅkīrṇā savitarkā Samāpattih*

There [in that *Samapatti*], when the word, the meaning and the knowledge, along with the confusion their intermixture generates, are reflected, each distinct from the other, then it is called *savitarka Samapatti.*

43. *Smṛtipariśudhau svarūpaśūnyeivā arthamātranibhāsa nirvitarkā*

When that *Samapatti* becomes completely cleansed of memory impregnations, and the mind becomes devoid of any form of its own, then it shines with the radiant reality of objectivity. This is called *nirvitarka Samapatti.*

44. *Etayaiva savicārā nirvicārā ca sūkṣma viṣayā vyākhyātā*

In the same way, when *Samapatti* reflects investigative thought and its subtle objects, both distinct from each other, it is called *savicara Samapatti.* And when even these are negated (because they are seen through), then the *Samapatti* that reflects this negation is called *nirvicara Samapatti.*

45. *Sūkṣmaviṣayatvanicā-liṅga-paryavasānam*
The subtleness of objects ends up in a state in which there are no distinguishing marks by which those objects can be identified.

46. *Tā eva Sabījān Samādhih*
These four kinds of *Samapattis* are called *Samadhi* with a seed [*sabija Samadhi*].

NOTES AND COMMENTS

It is necessary to take a few things into account to understand the significance of these Sutras.

Sutra 40 speaks of the sweep of the mind ranging from the tiniest particles to the boundless skies. This may appear to be fantastic. But if we follow the inner logic of the Sutras, right from Sutra 2 to Sutra 41, it may be possible for us to visualize the possibilities and potentialities inherent in the human mind, and capable of being actualized through the discipline of Yoga.

The inner logic of the Sutras runs as follows:

1. Sutra 2 speaks of *citta-vrtti-nirodha* and Sutra 4 speaks of *vrtti-sarupya.* This latter generates a river of conditional consciousness (*sansarapragbhara cittanadi*), in which men are born, inevitably come to grief, and then pass away. One who becomes aware of this senseless absurdity and the utter meaninglessness of life which it involves, halts for a moment to take stock of this senseless drifting. In this halt he perceives the fact that at the root of this senseless drifting lies the choice-making tendency with which man is born, and that this tendency works through built-in likes and dislikes. It is the movement of this choice-making tendency that lands man in the enslaving, confusing and corrupting prison-house of *vrtti-sarupya* – a home-made world of gratuitous identifications with *vrttis*. One who sees this fact opts in favour of not making choices, and then sees what happens. This negative act of not-choosing, with a view to stepping out of the prison-house of *vrtti-sarupya*, lands man in the discipline of Yoga.

2. The negative movement started by the negative act of not-choosing, discloses to one's view the following facts: that *vrttis* are of two kinds: painful and painless; that man tends to accept the painless and reject the painful; that this uncritical acceptance and rejection, out of which *vrtti-sarupya* is born, lands man in a way of life governed

by the five-fold *vrttis*; and that it is this way of life which forms the nature and structure of the conditioned psyche through *vrtti-sarupya*. Perception of this pattern of *vrtti-sarupya* as a whole, strengthens one in his resolve to keeps on with not-choosing. It is this perceptive resolve that discloses that *continuity* of *vrttis*, or the river of conditioned consciousness, is not a fact but a fiction. The fact is that *vrttis* are *discontinuous*; that, if one is attentive enough, one sees that in between two *vrttis* there comes an interval devoid of any movement of the mind. This is named as *sthiti* or the steady state of mind (Sutras 12 to 14). Energetic interest in this *sthiti* is called *abhyasa* (Sutra 13.).

3. *Abhyasa* discloses that the steady state comes, stays awhile, and passes away. This brings an awareness of the fact that there must be something within the mind which propels the movement of *vrttis*, despite one's having opted for not-choosing. One then discovers that words and impregnation of past experiences are the two factors, the combined operation of which, constituting a force brought into being by past choice, keeps the river of conditioned consciousness perpetually moving. This perception brings on state of total disillusionment (*vairagya*) regarding words and experiences. One therefore resolves not to have anything to do with them, and to stay on in a steady state devoid of or uninfluenced by words and experiences. This perception discloses an altogether new world in which the mind moves on without the help of words and experiences. This is called the world of *vasikara vairagya*.

4. The word *vasikara* is derived from the root *vas* turning to *vasi*, combined with the root *kr*. The dynamic combination of these two verbs means: 'to subdue, overcome, win over'. *Vairagya*, which negates the obsessive influence of words and experiences, brings into being a positive inner movement which goes on subduing and overcoming the past-propelled movement of *vrttis* which repeatedly disturbs the steady state of mind. This subduing and overcoming of the enslaving power of words and experiences results in negating the impregnations on the brain cell and the mind. And as these past impregnations (*smrti-samskara*) wear out and become inoperative, the mind becomes free, pure and crystal clear. The walls around it, built up by past impregnations, crumble down, along with all the accumulated rubbish and, therefore, the mind as it were spreads out and extends, as though it has no barriers or frontiers. It is such a free, pure and crystal clear mind that has an inherent power of penetrating into the innermost recesses of the psychosomatic organism of man,

on the one hand, and the objective world extending up to the boundless skies, on the other.

5. Sutra 40 describes the *vasikara* power of 'mind-in-*vairagya*'. It states that the steady state of mind, now cleansed off all the rubbish of past impregnations, acquires such a mighty sweep that it ranges from the tiniest particles of the body to the vastness of galaxies in the boundless skies. The process by which such a sweeping, penetrating and expanding power comes about is explained in Sutra 41.

Sutra 41 states that, as a result of the power of the *vasikara* movement, mind becomes pure and crystal clear. And, just as a pure crystal reflects the colours of objects brought in to its proximity, so also the mind, now becomes pure and clear, reflects the colours of the subtle interaction between man and the objective world. This interaction constantly goes on through the senses, although man caught up in *vrtti-sarupya* remains insensitive to it. Purity and clarity, which *vasikara vairagya* brings about, make the mind extraordinarily sensitive to everything that takes place within and without, every moment. Such a mind, therefore, reflects the 'receiver', the 'received' and the 'instruments of receiving', the senses – the combined operation of which keep man in constant interaction with the world in which he finds his being.

This extraordinarily reflective and highly sensitive state of mind is named as *Samapatti* in Sutra 41. *Samapatti* means 'meeting, encountering'. The entity called 'Man' and the entity called the 'world', inclusive of man, meet and encounter each other on the ground called *citta* or the mind. There is no man without mind; and there is no choice-making mind without man. Man and the world meet each other through the senses on the ground of mind. Here they react with or respond to each other. The built-in choice-making tendency of man disturbs, distorts and turns topsy-turvy the natural order of things. This generates inner tensions which seek outward expression. In Part II we shall see what the Yoga Sutras have to say on this matter. For the present we are concerned with the broad outlines of Yoga and *Samadhi*.

We have so far travelled from (a) *citta-vrtti-nirodha* to *sthiti*; (b) from *sthiti* to *vairagya*; and (c) from the *vasikara* power of *vairagya* to *Samapatti* – the reflecting state. Sutras 42 to 45 tell us that this *Samapatti* state of mind flowers into four kinds of *Samadhi*, all of which fall under the catagory of *sabiya Samadhi* (Sutra 46).

There is one more important point which has to be noted in

connection with *Samapatti*, the reflecting state. Mind in this state not only reflects everything that goes on as a result of the constant interaction between man and the world, but it also remains totally unsullied by what it reflects. It is like a pure crystal which reflects the colours of an object brought into its proximity, but which neither receives nor retains any stain on its body such as can be seen when the object is moved away from it. And even while reflecting the colours of an adjacent object, it absorbes no stain and remains wholly uninvolved in the colours it reflects. Mind in *Samapatti* behaves exactly like this. It reflects everything, within and without, but remains totally uncontaminated by such reflections. This is in sharp contrast with the *vrtti-sarupya* state. In this latter state the mind, for a split second, reflects the colours, but immediately gets identified with the choices made in respect of them. It therefore reflects nothing because the dirt of identifications destroys its reflectivity and renders it insensitive to 'what is'. The exact opposite of this is the case with the *Samapatti* state. *Samapatti* is thus a state of total transformation of the *vrtti-sarupya* state. Because of this transformation, whatever now enters into the crystal clear mind also undergoes transformation by the very power of pure perception.

Sutra 42 speaks of the first transformation that comes about. This is named as *savitarka Samapatti*. In this kind of *Samapatti* one sees the operation of words, their meanings and the knowledge they impart, along with the confusion that results through their intermixture. In this perception each of these three factors, along with their specific functions, is seen as distinct from the other two. Because of a very clear perception of these distinctions there is no room for confusion, which is invariably born of the mixing up of these three factors with each other. It is such confusion which leads to mistaking the word for the meaning, and vice versa. And since knowledge is nothing but a process of recognition of things through words and their conventional meanings, it also becomes a bewildering mess of confusion, full of inner and unnoticed contradictions. Again, since knowledge is always of the past, and thus a built-in-reaction to present perception, it is invariably tied up with words and their fixed meanings based on the impregnations of past experiences.

All this chaos and confusion is seen through and transcended in *savitarka Samapatti*. This is called *savitarka* because all knowledge obtained through words and their conventional meanings is basically inferential. *Tarka* means inference. And inference needs a referent embedded in the memory apparatus. The influence which this inferential knowledge exercises on the minds of men all over the world is so colossal, and the social prestige it enjoys is so aweful, that man's enslavement to it seems almost irremediable. *Savitarka Samapatti* liberates man from this stupefying enslavement.

Having seen through the nature and structure of inferential knowledge, one gets liberated from its tentacles. This freedom from inferential knowledge brings on a state of mind which is named as *nirvitarka Samapatti* – *Samapatti* devoid of *tarka* and inferential knowledge (Sutra 43). This is brought about by a process of negating all word-generated memory impregnations, on the basis of which the operation of recognition and inference generally works. The mind cleansed of all past impregnations, and the vessel of memory emptied of them, acquires a purity and clarity in which not recognition but pure perception prevails. In this state all inferential knowledge, along with words and their conventional meanings is seen as an impediment to direct perception of truth, or of things as they are.

Sutra 44 speaks of *savicara* and *nirvicara Samapatti.* When one is free from the tentacles of inferential knowledge, one begins to see things as they are in their existential radiance, without the agency of words and their conventional meanings. One then finds oneself in a state of free inquiry, an investigative thought process, which is *vicara.* This is distinct from all inferential processes.

In fact these latter have no place in *vicara* or free inquiry. In free inquiry one just observes what is, and never comes to any conclusion. Because to get caught up in conclusions, which necessarily involves choosing and inference, is to go back to the confusion and chaos. One therefore stays in a state of alert attention and just sees things as they are in their existential authenticity. Such pure seeing reveals the subtle elements which underlie things in their natural interaction with each other. Sensitivity is now so sharp and so penetrating that things and their subtle movements which have never been seen before, are now perceived as though in the light of inner illumination. This is *savicara Samapatti.* And when the subtle elements underlying the movements of things are seen, it happens that, just because they are seen as they are, they dissolve into a state of being in which these subtle things lose all marks by which they could be identified. And, as there is now nothing to identify, the movement of *vicara* comes to an end. This state is called *nirvicara Samapatti.*

All these four kinds of *Samapattis* fall under one head, called *sabija*

Samadhi. The question here is: why is this *Samadhi* associated with a 'seed' (*bija*)? What exactly is indicated by the word *bija* or seed? How can *nirvitarka Samapatti*, in which things are seen as they are in their existential radiance, be a product of any seed? And again, how can *nirvicara Samapatti*, in which subtle elements underlying all massive objects are seen to dissolve in a kind of emptiness of space, be said to be associated or supported by any 'seed'?

The following Sutras throw some light on these disturbing questions.

9
From Seed-based to Seedless Samadhi

Sutras 47 to 51

47. *Nirvicāra-vaiśāradye-adhyātma-prasādah*
Proficiency in the state devoid of any thought-movement results in inward gracious felicity of disposition.

48. *Ṛtaṁbharā tatra prajñā*
There [in that inward graciousness] dwells wisdom, or intelligence charged with reality.

49. *Ṣrutānumāna prajñābhyāmanya-viṣayā viśeṣārthatvāt*
This wisdom, or reality-charged intelligence, is distinct from the intelligence associated with words and inferences, because it signifies something unique and extraordinary.

50. *Tajjah saṅskāro-nyasaṅskāra-pratibaṅdhī*
Impressions born of it oppose and eliminate all other binding impregnations.

51. *Tasyāpi nirodhe sarvanirodhān-nirbījah samādhih*
The ending even of these [new] impressions results in the ending of everything. That which emerges out of this ending of everything is *nirbija* [seedless] *Samadhi*.

NOTES AND COMMENTS

We are now at the end of the journey. We started with *citta-vrtti-nirodha*; and we are now being told that seedless *Samadhi* is the end. Throughout this journey our attention was drawn to *citta* (mind), the ground on which all the battles of life are fought. The battles are between man at one end, and the world, full of a bewildering variety of objects, including man, at the other end. The history of man is the history of the turns and twists these battles take from time to time, from epoch to epoch. It is mind that makes or unmakes man. Mind caught up in *vrtti-sarupya* (identifications with choices) unmakes man; and mind totally disentangled from *vrtti-sarupya* establishes man in his existential identity. To realize his true identity, or to get lost in alienation – this is the central issue in man's life. And this issue is the subject-matter of the discipline of Yoga.

In the last chapter we saw the stages through which the mind passes, once one opts for *citta-vrtti-nirodha*. The last stage is the stage of mind devoid of any movement in any direction (Sutra 46). This is named as seed-based *Samadhi*. The Sutras now before us deal with the last and total transformation of the mind. It is said to be a transformation from a seed-based *Samadhi* to a seedless *Samadhi*.

The question is: what is signified by the word *bija* or the seed? Yoga speaks of two seeds that grow in the soil of mind: (i) the seed contained in *vrtti-sarupya* (identifications), which grows into a wild and anarchic forest of tensions, conflicts, chaos and unending sorrow; (ii) the seed contained in *vrtti-nirodha* (steady state), which grows and flowers into a seed-based *Samadhi* – a state of being, devoid of any movement of mind in any direction. This is a state pregnant with the entire energy of man's being, which, before one opted for not making choices, was dissipated and wasted in tensions, repeatedly and inevitably ending up in unending misery.

One is now on the threshold of a new transformation. The movement towards this transformation is explained in the Sutras now before us.

Sutra 47 speaks of the first stir towards this transformation. It says that a mind devoid of any thought movement acquires by itself a proficiency, a new-born capacity to remain in this motionless state, without any effort. This results in a disposition of vulnerable felicity which responds to everything, within and without, with an easy and beautiful gracefulness. It seeks nothing. It finds in this gracefulness the very vibration of Life, which it had never experienced before. There is now a graceful response to everything and reaction to nothing.

Sutra 48 speaks of an upsurge of an altogether new kind of intelligence, which has emerged from the unfathomable depths of one's being. This new intelligence is charged with the energy of reality. This reality is named as *Rtam*. *Rtam* is that mysterious something which comes from the 'Great Unknown' and disappears in it, from moment to moment, as though the incoming and outgoing moments are the incoming and outgoing breaths of Reality itself. *Rtam* is that which always 'is', but whose rhythm of breathing appears to take the form of 'is' and 'is not'. *Rtam* is an ancient Vedic word which is described as a movement having a centre everywhere and circumference nowhere. All bodies, all objects in this world have, each one of them, a centre and a circumference. To have a centre is to get enclosed in a circumference. On the physical plane, it is the nucleus forming the positively charged central portion constituting the main mass of an atom, around which electrons, one or many, move with tremendous speed to form a tough circumference. On the psychic plane, it is the central core of the psyche constituting an unconscious force which reacts to external or internal pressures in such a manner as to preserve and protect itself through a tough circumference built up of choice-born concepts of comfort, pleasure and self-gratification. Man, as a mind-made entity, calls this central core of his being the 'I' or the 'me'. It becomes the final authority to judge or evaluate anything, the final arbiter in the matter of acceptance or rejection, agreement or disagreement. When it abdicates this position of being the final authority, it seeks refuge in the authority of a book or a guru, or of a leader with a large following.

The discipline of Yoga tells us that this central core of one's psyche is nothing else but a very tough complex of *vrtti-sarupya*. Until and unless this central core is broken up through *vrtti-nirodha* (not-choosing and remaining in a steady state), there can be no perception of truth or reality, so far as it relates vitally to one's identity. Identification is identity sold out for a song. Therefore, one who opts for the discipline of Yoga is launched on a voyage which lands him in *Samadhi*. *Samadhi* is a state in which all the emotional and conceptual attributes which are attached to identity, like borrowed feathers, fall off and vanish in nothingness. One becomes like an entity having no form of its own, and yet an entity full of the energy that is life. It is now 'Life itself' that takes over one's identity, in the sense that between identity and Life there now remains neither space nor time nor causation.

In the seed-based *Samadhi* there is the recollection of one's act of not-choosing, which brought one to the discipline of Yoga, but it is now a recollection which is one with the state brought on by *nirvicara Sampatti* (Sutras 44, 45). It has no movement. But its very existence operates as a seed with which *Samadhi* gets associated. It is like an immobilized sense of 'I-am-ness' living in association with *Samadhi*. And this immobilized sense of I-am-ness is the seed. Hence *sabija-Samadhi*.

But with the dawning of new intelligence charged by Reality

(*Rtam*), it is now an altogether different world, having no dimensions. It is as though the rocket of new intelligence explodes and hurtles one into this dimensionless world of Reality.

In this world of reality the old intelligence associated with words, verbalizations and inferences has no place whatsoever because it is seen as utterly irrelevant to reality, with which alone the newly dawned intelligence is concerned (Sutra 49). The operation of this new intelligence burns up whatever residue may still be lingering in the mind of impregnations coming from the beginningless past. Mind so totally cleansed of the past, and with nothing left now in respect of which any decision, negative or positive, needs to be made, spontaneously flowers into a seedless *Samadhi.*

Here ends Part I, called *Samadhi Pada.* It has given us a broad vision of the discipline of Yoga – how it begins and how it ends. But even so, one realizes that one is still for away from that state of beatitude called *Samadhi.* Patanjali, therefore, takes us to Part II in which he expounds *Kriya Yoga*, the Yoga of action. It is the way illuminated by action born of the perception of what Yoga stands for.

PART TWO
Sadhana Pada

1
Yoga in Action

SUTRAS 1 AND 2

1. *Tapah svādhyāyeṣvarapraṇidhānāni kriyā yogah*
Austerity, self-study and God-awareness, together constitute Yoga in action.

2. *Samādhi-bhāvanārthah, Kleśa-tanūkaranārthaśca*
It promotes meditation flowering into *Samadhi* and minimizes tensions.

NOTES AND COMMENTS

One who has listened attentively to what has been expounded in Part I, would naturally tend to live in a manner consistent with the awareness of what is signified by Yoga or *Samadhi.*

To live is to act from moment to moment. Life is action in which the organism of a sentient being is involved in its totality. Man however, is a sentient being who tends to live and act fragmentarily, and not totally. He does so because he is free to pick and choose. So to pick and choose is to break the totality, that is life, into fragments; it tends to equate a fragment with the whole. Fragments have meaning only in relation to the whole, as integral parts of the whole. To opt for a fragment and ignore the whole is to miss the very essence of life. It is this initial mistake which lands man in a mind-made world of ideational dreams that are reduced to ashes by the very touch of the existential and the real. The contradiction between the ideational and the existential inevitably results in tensions, conflict, confusion, chaos and misery.

To live in a manner consistent with the awareness of what is signified by Yoga is to live and act totally, and not fragmentarily. Such action, which in fact is life in its existential authenticity, is called *Kriya Yoga.*

Kriya means action. And *Yoga* means *citta-vrtti-nirodha*. Hence, action that is born of *citta-vrtti-nirodha* is *Kriya Yoga*. One who understands this naturally tends to live a life that is charged with the awareness of Yoga. But as soon as he does so, he finds himself confronted with difficulties. These difficulties are the products of past-propelled *vrttis*, which inevitably generate tensions between the ideational and the existential. Despite the fact that one understands what is implied by Yoga and the action that is consistent with it, one's psychosomatic organism, which is a product of the past, continues to function under the compulsive weight of past impregnations (*samskara*). All difficulties are born out of a basic tension between, on the one hand, the understanding of Yoga, which is in the active present, and on the other hand the continuity of the past-propelled *vrttis*. It is to meet this predicament that *Kriya Yoga* is propounded in this Part II of the Yoga Darsanam.

Sutra 1 equates *Kriya Yoga* with three things: *tapas*, *svadhyaya* and *isvarapranidhana*, i.e. austerity, self-study and God-awareness. It is interesting to note that in Part I the word Yoga is also equated with three things, namely, *citta, vrtti*, and *nirodha*. These three things have to be taken together, and not separately. And since Yoga means *citta-vrtti-nirodha*, action that is Yoga must be born of *citta-vrtti-nirodha*. And it is this action that is now being equated with *tapas, svadhyaya* and *isvarapranidhana*. Obviously, there must be a vital connection between these three things and *citta-vrtti-nirodha*. We shall presently see the nature of this connection.

The word *tapas* is derived from the root *tap* which means 'to shine'. It also means, 'to be hot, to be intense'. Intensity of being (austerity), high sensitivity to what is happening within and without, is *tapas*. This comes about naturally when one understands what is signified by Yoga. What happens within and without happens on the ground of *citta*. The senses bring the data from the outside world within one's being. And *citta*, which receives the data, gets agitated by them. This agitation excites the past impregnations on the memory or the brain cells, and one reacts to the sense-data in terms of these past impregnations; that is to say, in terms of past experiences, and of the words which enshrine them. But when one understands what is signified by Yoga, the whole of this past-propelled process of reacting to what happens, within and without, is seen to be productive of inner contradiction, tension, conflict, confusion, chaos and misery. One, therefore, rejects the past and opts for not-choosing. This rejection holds back the energy of one's being in a state devoid of *vrttis* (*nirodha*). The energy that was being dissipated and wasted in identification with *vrttis*, is now held back in its totality. Naturally, therefore, it acquires tremendous intensity. This intensity of the energy of one's being is what is signified by the word *tapas*.

All other traditional meanings associated with the word *tapas* have to be discarded for the right understanding of *Kriya Yoga*. Tradition associates mortification of body and mind with the meaning of the word *tapas*. This is totally inconsistent with the whole theme of the Yoga Sutras. Yoga means *citta-vrtti-nirodha*, as explained in Part I. As such, it cannot possibly have anything to do with wilful and egocentric mortification of body or mind. On the contrary, so to mortify body or mind is to intensify and multiply tensions, which generate impediments to Yoga, as mentioned in Sutras 29 to 31 of Part I. All tensions originate primarily from identification with *vrttis* (*vrttisarupya*, I-4). Negation of identification brings about ,*vrtti-nirodha*, which is the state of mind in which Yoga and *Samadhi* blossom. Therefore, the word *tapas* cannot mean mortification of body or mind. It signifies intensity of one's being which results as a natural consequence of *citta-vrtti-nirodha*.This intensity purifies *citta*, just as gold mixed with earth is purified by the intense heat of a blazing fire. Hence *tapas* becomes an integral part of *Kriya Yoga*.

The word *svadhyaya* is a compound of two words: *sva* and *adhyaya*. *Adhyaya* means 'learning, studying'. And *sva* means 'one's own'. '*Svadhyaya*', therefore, means 'to learn about one's own self'. How does one learn about oneself? Books and what one hears from others may give us some knowledge or information about things. But the conditioned consciousness always forces us to pick and choose what we like and reject what we dislike from among the books, or from among the words of others however learned they may be. Consequently, neither books nor words nor experiences, whether one's own or of others, can ever help one to learn about one's own self (*sva*). The only way to learn about oneself is to observe the play of *vrttis* as they emerge as reactions to whatever comes within one's mind. Such observation of one's own *vrttis* has got to be made in a state of choiceless awareness to be objective or realistic. This is *svadhyaya* or self-study. *Svadhyaya* is thus related to *vrttis*. And this self-study brings about purification of *vrttis*. As one observes them, one learns to see how they arise, what motivates them, where they lead, and so on. And as one observes choicelessly, one sees that the *vrttis* get deprived of their power to generate tensions. They are thus purified, and one's identification with them comes to an end. The purification of *vrttis*, which self-study thus brings about, liberates one from their tentacles.

It is pertinent to note here that, just as *tapas* purifies *citta* (mind), *syadhyaya* purifies *vrttis* (movements of the mind), and liberates one from their bondage.

The third and the last element of *Kriya Yoga* is *isvarapranidhana* (God-awareness). We have seen what this word means and implies in our comments on Sutras 23 to 29 of Part I. The point that deserves special attention in this connection is that *isvarapranidhana* is vitally associated with *nirodha*, a state devoid of *vrttis*. The word 'God', as defined in Part I-24, necessarily points to a state of being 'untouched by tensions, tension-born activity, activity-born fruit, and fruit-born impregnations on the psyche'. All this is possible only in a state devoid of *vrttis*, which is *nirodha*. The presence of God can only be felt in a state devoid of egocentric activities of the mind and body. This is the state called *abhyasa* and it is born of *nirodha*. God dwells in that 'Great Void' devoid of *vrttis*. His presence may be felt only in the Void, and nowhere else. This is indicated even by the root meaning of the word *pranidhana*. This is a compound of the prefix *pra* with *nidhana. Nidhana* means 'a place where anything is placed', and *pra* means 'with intensity'. *Isvara-pra-nidha-na* thus means 'the space, a void, full of the intensity of Being, where God dwells'.

We thus discover that whereas Yoga is *citta-vrtti-nirodha, Kriya Yoga* is *tapas-svadhyaya-isvarapranidhana. Tapas* is related to purification of *citta*; *svadhyaya* is related to purification of *vrttis*; and *isvarapranidhana* is related to *nirodha. Kriya Yoga* is thus a process or action integrally associated with what is signified by Yoga. It is action born of Yoga. Hence the phrase *Kriya Yoga.*

Kriya Yoga is not a matter of doing but of being aware of everything that one may be doing. This Yogic awareness purifies all egocentric activities, from which the poisonous touch of egotism or petty selfishness is thus totally eliminated. It is in this manner that the past-propelled egocentric way of living, born of a conditioned consciousness, is radically transformed by *Kriya Yoga* into a Yogic way of living in the present.

Sutra 2 tells us what happens as result of *Kriya Yoga*. Two things happen: on the one hand, through meditation (*bhavana*) one moves closer and closer to *Samadhi*; and, on the other, one's entanglement in tensions (*klesas*) is reduced to such an extent that the *klesas* no longer act as impediments.

What these tensions (*klesas*) are, and how their elimination comes about, is explained in the following Sutras.

2
The Nature of Tensions

SUTRAS 3 TO 9

3. *Avidyāsmitārāgadvesābhiniveśāh pañca Kleśāh*
The tensions are five, namely, unawareness, the sense of I-am-ness, attachment to pleasure, hatred of pain, and a dogged clinging to self-perpetuation.

4. *Avidyā kṣetramuttareṣāṁ prasupta-tanuviccinnodārāṇāṁ*
Avidya [unawareness] is the field in which the succeeding four tensions [Klesa] take root and appear in four forms: *viz.* the hidden or unconscious mind; mind taking interest in trivialities; mind splitting up into fragmentary interest in various things; and mind spreading over the whole field of individual life through fragmentary occupations.

5. *Anityāśuchidukhānātmasu nityaśuchisukhātmakhyātiravidyā*
Avidya is [self-centred] knowledge [or vision] in which one assumes what in fact is transient to be permanent; what in fact is impure; and what in fact is painful to be pleasurable.

6. *Dṛkdarśanaśaktyorekātmatevāsmitā*
To assume that energy that is 'seeing' and energy that is the 'seen' are one and the same thing [though in fact they are two distinct entities] is a tension called *asmita* [the sense of I-am-ness–self-centredness].

7. *Sukhānuśayī rāgah*
Slumbering in pleasure [under the influence of a lingering memory of pleasurable past experiences] is a tension called *raga.*

8. *Dukkhānuśavī dveṣah*
Slumbering in pain [under the influence of a lingering memory of painful past experiences] is a tension called *dvesa.*

9. *Svarasavāhī viduṣo-pi tanvanubandhah abhiniveśah*
Continuous self-generative interest in self-perpetuation, which

is bound up with the body and is found even among the learned, is a tension called *abhinivesa*.

NOTES AND COMMENTS

These and the following Sutras bring us face to face with the central paradox of human life. Man lives with a feeling of absolute certainty that the world in which he has his being is just a matter of his personal knowledge; but sooner or later he discovers, that the entire structure of his world-view, built on the basis of personal knowledge, crumbles into pieces at the very first shock of reality. Even so, he doggedly clings to personal knowledge as the only means available to him to establish a meaningful relationship with the objective world. He realizes that personal knowledge may be limited, to begin with and, therefore, inadequate to comprehend the reality of the world in its totality; but he persists in the belief that its limitations can be eliminated as he gathers more and more knowledge by observation, analysis, experiment, and by refinement of his instruments – all of which enable him to build up a world-view (*darsana*), which grows better and more adequate from age to age. This assumption of absolute certainty about the world-view based on personal knowledge, and capable of expanding limitlessly, is the bedrock on which the historical view of the man–world relationship is founded. And through the ages it has acquired such a respectability that no one must challenge it except at the cost of being socially ostracized.

The discipline of Yoga challenges this deeply entrenched assumption. It points out that personal knowledge, however expansive it may be and no matter how far it may be justified and fortified by observation, analysis, experiment and systematized thought, is still basically illusive or false. This is so because in order to be objective and realistic observation must be pure and crystal clear. It must not be distracted, deflected, or distorted by anything, within or without, and the act of observation itself must be free, and not impeded by any motive or preconceived notion because any motive or preconceived notion is bound to influence and colour, and thus distort it. Nothing which has been observed through a distorted vision, and later analysed, experimented upon and put into the framework of a systematized thought-pattern, can ever correspond to objective reality. The fact of the matter is that a conditioned mind, that is a mind encumbered with past impregnations and the built-in likes and dislikes which inevitably result from them, is basically incapable of pure observation. As later Sutras point out, every act born of a conditioned mind is an act of born of tensions which colour man's world-view. And acts born of tensions (including the acts of observation, analysis, experiment and systematization of thoughts) are acts that must inevitably generate further tensions, and so on *ad infinitum*. Therefore, say the Sutras, tensions must cease for observation to be pure and crystal clear and capable of seeing things as they are in their existential authenticity.

The basic tension with which man is born is called *avidya* (unawareness of 'what is'). It is basic because to remain unaware of 'what is' is to bring into being a tension between 'what actually is' and 'what one thinks it is'. All the other tensions are born of this basic tension. These built-in tensions, which manifest themselves in the form of instinctive tendencies (*vrttis*), weave the very fabric of man's consciousness. There is no escape from the tentacles of these tensions unless and until one is able to see, first and foremost, the fact of one's imprisonment in them; and secondly, the fact that the built-in tendencies (*vrttis*) generating tensions also carry with them the freedom to choose. But one cannot just wish these tensions and their tentacles away. One cannot think oneself out of them. In short, one can do nothing to be free of their clutches because every egocentric act is an act which originates from built-in tensions. Therefore, the only way open to us is the way of freedom exercised in the direction of not making choices. Freedom so exercised is alone capable of removing all mind-made obstructions to pure seeing. Therefore, say the Sutras, tensions must cease for pure perception to be. It is pure perception alone that can enable man to see things as they are in their existential authenticity. It is such free and pure vision (*darsana*) that puts man into intimate relationship with the world of radiant objectivity.

The paradox of human life is born of a conflict between knowledge or vision in its purity, on the one hand, and knowledge generated by personal predilections, on the other. Knowledge or vision born of personal predilections is called *avidya-khyati* in Sutra 5. This is knowledge born of tensions (*klesa*) which generate chain-reactions resulting in unending sorrow and misery (Sutra 15).

Sutras 3 to 9 explain the nature of the five major tensions. The first and primary tension is called *avidya*. This word means unawareness of 'what is'. It is derived from the root *vid* which means 'to know, understand, learn find out, ascertain, discover'. The prefix *a* means negation. Therefore, not caring to know, learn, understand, find out, ascertain and discover 'what is', is to remain in a state of unawareness, and to go on living with a self-centred consciousness which is unaware of what is, within and without, is *avidya.* The root *vid* also means 'to be, to exist'. *Avidya* would thus mean knowledge of that which has no existence in fact, but which is ideationally assumed to exist, and as such becomes an object of knowledge. This assumption is born of the memory of past experiences impregnated on the mind or the brain cells. All knowledge stimulated by memory is essentially of the past which is dead and gone for ever and which no longer exists in the active present. Even so, it is gratuitously assumed to be still in existence. Knowledge based on such an assumption purports to impart continuity of existence to things which in fact have ceased to exist.

Taking all these subtle shades of meanings into account, *avidya* is defined as 'knowledge or vision (*khyati*) in which one assumes that to be permanent which in fact is transient' (Sutra 5). *Avidya* in this Sutra is said to be a *Khyati.* This word is derived from the root *khya*, which means 'to tell, declare, communicate'. One may 'tell, declare, communicate' what is factual or what is ideationally assumed to be, but which in fact, is not so. This latter is *avidya-khyati.* This *khyati* is a matter of naming, verbalization, declaration in words, with a view to communicating something. It has nothing to do with what actually exists, within or without. It is a matter of ideation, imagination and articulation in words. It is a declaration. Everything that exists declares itself to others, by the very fact of its existence. A tiger or a snake declares, by its very existence, that one may go near it only at one's own risk. Man, being a 'language animal', declares what he is through words. But words are not things. They indicate things which may or may not exist. But man naturally becomes a captive of words which he tends to equate with knowledge or reality. And this is *avidya-khyati*, or illusory knowledge on which man's whole view of the world is generally based. His knowledge or his vision, or his world-view thus gets turned upside-down. He assumes that to be permanent which in fact is transient, that to be pure which in fact is impure, and that to be pleasurable which in fact is painful. Is there a pleasure which does not turn into pain, disillusionment, frustration? But, carried away by the waves of momentary pleasures, in utter unawareness of the facts of the existential situation, man tends to get established in *avidya* and therefore assumes that to be permanent which in fact is ephemeral. In this way, the whole structure of human life gets motivated by false notions of what is permanent and what is ephemeral, what is pure and what is impure, and what is pleasure and what is pain.

Avidya thus becomes the soil in which all psychic tensions take root and shoot up in many forms to entangle man in their tentacles. The first tension that gets rooted in this manner in man's psyche is the sense of I-am-ness (*asmita*). This sense of 'I-ness' would not come into being in the absence of *avidya*. In a state of awareness one refers to everything one sees as 'it', including man. It is, therefore, unawareness that gives man the sense of I-ness. This sense of I-ness connotes an indivisible unit of existence. It renders man utterly unaware of the fact that, as an entity, he is made up of two distinct energies, which can never become one. These two energies must always remain distinct from one another, although they may coexist in the same body, as in fact they do. Man is both the 'seer' and the 'seen' at one and the same place and time. It is not only possible but imperative for man to see the fact that the 'seer' can never become the 'seen', and vice versa. To interchange these two distinct energies, by mixing them up ideationally, is to land oneself in confusion. These two energies interact with each other from moment to moment. And the very fact of this interaction necessarily implies that they must ever remain two distinct forces of being and living. In fact, every human experience, true or false, is a product of existential interaction between these two eternal varieties. Without seeing and accepting this fact, there can be no clear experiencing of anything, and therefore no talk about or discovery of what is real and what is unreal.

Therefore, the sense of I-am-ness is a product of unawareness of what is (*avidya*). It abides in man's being in the form of a deep slumber (*prasupta*) or unconsciousness masquerading as consciousness. This is the nature of egocentric consciousness. The centre, the 'I', becomes the most important factor in man's life, and overrides all other aspects of life. It is this ideational centre which drives man, blindfold, to choose what he likes, and discard what he dislikes. He tends to like what the memory of past experiences tells him is pleasurable. And he tends to dislike what the memory of past experiences tells him is painful. The former is a tension called *raga* and the latter is a tension called *dvesa*.

All three (*asmita, raga* and *dvesa*) are tensions because they carry with them a contradiction between the ideational and the existential. The fifth and the last tension is called *abhinivesa.* This dominates man's life to such an extent that it overshadows everything else. It is a dogged clinging to one's instinctive interest in self-perpetuation, with a relish which is difficult to discard. One cannot relish one's disappearance and reduction to nothingness. One cannot, even for a moment, relish loss of self-importance, whatever view others may take about oneself. Any threat to one's sense of self-importance seems as annihilating as death. Interest in one's importance is regarded by man as the very essence of life. One always says to oneself, 'What else is there for the human individual to live for and die for?' This sense of self-importance sometimes transcends even the prospect of death. Quite a few men in every apoch have gambled away their lives for some cause, in which a dogged belief gave them an added sense of self-importance and self-perpetuation.

It is necessary to note one point in connection with the tensions. Sutra 4 refers to four forms which the four tensions born of *avidya* take. *Asmita* takes the form of unconsciousness masquerading as self-consciousness. *Raga* takes the form of pleasure in the petty things of life. *Dvesa* takes the form of splitting up life into a number of fragments which are perpetually at war with each other. And *abhinivesa* takes the form of a feeling of self-perpetuation, which spreads all over and envelops in its tentacles all aspects and urges of life.

As will be seen presently, it is with *abhinivesa* that one has to begin when one sees the necessity of freeing one's mind from all tensions. The Yogic way which leads to freedom from all tensions is called *pratiprasav* or counter-creativity. This forms the subject matter of the following Sutras.

3
Pratiprasava – The Way Out

SUTRAS 10 TO 17

10. *Te pratiprasava heyāh sūkṣmāh*
They [tensions] have to be removed by means of counter-creativity [*pratiprasava*] because they are very subtle.

11. *Dhyāna-heyāstadvṛttayah*
Ideational movements triggered by them can be removed through meditation [*dhyana*].

12. *Kleśamūlah karmāśayah dṛṣṭā- dṛṣṭa-janma vedanīyah*
The individual psyche is an activity-oriented residue having its roots in tensions; its operations are capable of being observed in this life through experiences; and its continuity in the life to come can also be understood in the same way.

13. *Sati mūle tadvipāko jātyāyurbhogāh*
The species, its life-duration and what it has to experience–these three are the products of the tensions-ridden psyche or mind-stuff (inherited by individuals).

14. *Te Chādaparitāpaphalāh puṇyāpuṇyahetutvāt*
Experiences of delight and of overpowering anguish are the results of actions motivated by either good or evil intentions, as the case may be.

15. *Pariṇāmatāpasaṁskārdukkhairguṇavṛtti-virodhātccava dukkhameva sarvaṁ vivekinah*
The fact that all is sorrow is understood by one having a discerning intelligence; he sees that this is so because cause–effect sequences resulting in agony get impregnated on the mind-stuff in the form of memories of sorrowful experiences; and also because the threefold energies [*gunas*] of nature, being mutually opposed to each other, generate tensions of which the mind-stuff is a product.

16. *Hevaṁ dukkhamanāgataṁ*
Sorrow that is yet to come can be discarded.
17. *Draṣṭṛdṛśyayoh saṁvogo heyahetuh*
Awareness of the fact that the contact between the 'seer' and the 'seen' is at the root of sorrow enables one to discard it.

NOTES AND COMMENTS

These Sutras reveal the *raison d'être* underlying tensions (*klesa*), within and without. Everything that is seen by man as existing is in fact a product of the primeval contact (*sanyoga*) between two energies: the 'seer' and the 'seen' (Sutra 17). But man remains unaware of this basic fact which underlies all existence. This unawareness of 'what is', the *sanyoga* or contact between two distinct primeval energies, is *avidya* (Sutra 24). And it is the continuity of *avidya* operating in the human organism, which induces man to assume that he, along with his body, is the 'seer' and all the rest is the 'seen'. He ignores the fact that his body is also an object that he can see, like any other object and so it too is part of the 'seen'. He further ignores the fact that 'seeing' implies and necessitates two things – the 'seer' and that which can be 'seen'. And since his body obviously falls in the category of the 'seen' it can never be the 'seer'. What then is the 'seer', quite apart from the body and everything that remains observable, the 'seen'? Man never cares to halt awhile to pursue this inquiry to the very end. This lack of care, awareness, attention, lands him in a tension called *asmita* (Sutra 6). And it is through the eyes of *asmita* that man looks at the world and his life. It is only when this confused 'seeing' repeatedly ends in sorrow (*dukkha*) that man is shaken to his very foundations. Few, however, care to face this upheaval. Most tend to seek easy ideational escapes and go along the old way determined by *avidya* and *asmita*, despite repeated experiences of sorrow and despair. But those few who halt and dare to face sorrow as the very condition of their existence, launch themselves on a new voyage – a quest for identity (*swarupa*).

Such a quest becomes a point of total departure from the past. Man now faces sorrow (*dukkha*) as being the inevitable consequence of the past-propelled and blind way of living. Sorrow now becomes the 'seen' – the end-product of time and temporality. Sorrow, as the very agony of existence, now begins to operate as the only *link* between him, as the 'seer', and the whole of existence as the 'seen'. This link is the newly discovered umbilical chord that joins him with Mother Nature. Nature sustains him, but only in and through misery. If this misery, this agony of existence, is to end, the umbilical chord that joins man with nature must be broken. It is like breaking the umbilical chord that has to be cut to set the child free from the body of the mother. In the same way, the 'seer' and the 'seen' must be separated into two distinct forces of existence which in fact they always are. The contact (*sanyoga*) operating through *asmita* must be seen as an interaction between two distinct energies, the 'seer' and the 'seen', which can never be one and the same thing. This perception leads to a clear understanding that *asmita* must end for pure perception to be.

It is this pure perception which makes man a *vivekin* (Sutra 15). *Viveka* means discerning intelligence; intelligence that is always capable of clearly distinguishing between the 'seer' and the 'seen' and never confusing the two. It is the light of this existential intelligence that illuminates a new path, a new movement, leading to the ending of tensions, unawareness of which repeatedly lands man in confusion, conflict, chaos and misery. This new, self-luminous movement is named as *Pratiprasava* in Sutra 10.

Sutra 10 says that tensions, which are very subtle, have to be discarded; and the only way they can be discarded is the way of *Pratiprasava*. This word is made up of *prasava* with the prefix *prati*. *Prasava* means 'begetting, generation, procreation'. And *prati* means 'in opposition to, against, counter'. Nature procreates everything, including the human species. Man is a product of this procreative power of nature. But man is the only animate being that is capable of being conscious of this procreative power of nature. It is because of this that modern anthropologists are driven by the very logic of evolution to describe man as 'evolution becomes conscious of itself'. To be so conscious or aware is to be a 'seer', one who perceives the whole of the objective world, the 'seen', as the product of nature. This extraordinary power of perception is unique to man. It is a power or energy without an attribute of quality or quantity with which all objects of nature are endowed. The 'seer' can never be the 'seen', the object, the observed. Neither can it be the 'subject' endowed with certain characteristics, the result of conditioning. This extraordinary energy that is 'pure seeing' is capable of penetrating and going to the very roots of everything that is observable or the 'seen'.

When man has become aware of this energy that is 'pure seeing', as being that unique thing which distinguishes his humanity from the whole of the animate and inanimate world he finds himself in an extraordinary state. The phenomena which are capable of making man aware of this extraordinary energy called 'seer' or 'pure seeing' are sorrow, anguish and existential despair. This is what is stated in Sutra 15. The shock of experiencing reality places man in this critical position. In this state the entire past becomes meaningless, and the future a total and impenetrable darkness. This is a revolutionary situation because it transcends time and temporality. The inevitable sequences of past–present–future, in which the mind is caught up become meaningless, if not utterly absurd. Sorrow, anguish, despair – a state of existential agony – becomes the only link between man and the rest of the world. If man does not seek ideational and false escapes from this existential situation, then he remains face to face with it, and accepts it as the reality of his life and being, without any inner tension. And since he refuses to run after any escapes, and remains steadfast facing the existential situation, time comes to a stop. It is like stopping the world which was set going by *vrittisarupya*, *avidya* and *asmita*, with which one moved willy-nilly through identification with *vrttis*.

The movement of *Pratiprasava* is not a movement of time. It looks at everything which time has put together and sees through it down to its very roots. If time and nature are procreative (*prasavatmaka*) *Pratiprasava* is also creative but runs counter to procreation. Hence 'counter-creative' – not a very happy rendering in English. It has to be understood in and through action that is Yoga (*Kriya Yoga*). If one does not move along with the action of pure perception, the phrase will remain devoid of any meaning.

One who understands the inner logic of these Sutras is equipped with new eyes to look at himself and the world and at the interaction that constantly goes on between the two. His first glance then falls on *abhinivesa* – the end-product of tensions. He sees how the feeling of self-importance always seeks self-perpetuation, and wants to impart permanence to what in fact is ephemeral. Every thought, every feeling or desire and every activity of man is dominated by a sense of self-importance. Everything in this wide world must subserve the ends of self-importance, as though one were at the very centre of this vast and mysterious universe. The entire world view of man is thus coloured by this sense of self-importance. The world is good or bad, true or false, beautiful or ugly but only in terms of self-importance. Even the ultimate reality of the world, whatever it may be, must conform to the demands and desires of man's self-importance to be meaningful or otherwise. One thus discovers that not truth nor falsehood, good nor evil, reality nor illusion, but self-perpetuating self-importance (*svarasavahi*), bound to one's body (*tanvanubandhah*), ever remains the decisive factor in man's life. And this utter stupidity appears to him natural and spontaneous.

Once this nature and structure of *abhinivesa* is clearly seen, one becomes aware that it is because of identification with this tension (understood not as a tension but as the undisputable existence of 'I-ness'), that man tends to be jealous, competitive, ambitious, aggressive and destructive, and thus becomes a victim of the rat-race in which mankind has been involved throughout all its history. Human history has so far been the history of this rat-race which masquerades as the march of progress through time; and man forgets that this 'progress through time' has at base been nothing other than the handiwork of *abhinivesa*.

Pratiprasava thus demolishes the citadel of *abhinivesa*, exposing to view its utter horror. This perception brings one face to face with *dvesa*, a congenital feeling of hatred of everything that hurts one's sense of self-importance – a feeling of being hurt when nursed within takes the self-justifying form of *abhinivesa*. The exposure of *dvesa* brings one face to face with *raga*, a lingering remembrance of pleasurable experiences. One sees how it feeds the sense of self-importance, and ultimately goes to strengthen *abhinivesa*. A little affront to *raga*, coming from the external world, suddenly turns it into *dvesa* – a hatred of everything that threatens *raga*. *Raga* is thus seen to be just the other side of the coin – the coin having two faces, one of *raga* and the other of *dvesa*.

One is now face to face with the bare I-am-ness (*asmita*) devoid of *raga-dvesa-abhinivesa*. This I-ness sees; but it also sees the stupidity of saying 'I see'. It sees that the energy of seeing makes one aware of the objective world, *the seen*. It just happens. One cannot make it happen or not happen. It is there – the 'seer' and the 'seen' constantly interacting with each other, and creating an ever fresh, ever mysterious relationship. One sees the fact that 'to be is to be related'. There is no *being* without *relatedness* although the latter remains a mystery. One asks: what is relatedness? And one is unable to answer, for it is a relationship between the 'seer' and the 'seen' in which the sense of 'I-am-ness' has no place. To super-impose 'I-ness' in between the two, is to mask a fact with a fiction, that is, to cover up 'what is', the existential, with the ideational – the choice-making propensity centred in 'I-am-ness'. To interpose 'I-am-ness' (*asmita*) between the two unknowns – the 'seer' and the 'seen' – is to move in a direction which inevitably lands one in the prison-house of *raga-dvesa-abhinivesa*. But If one does not move, what happens? The interaction between the 'seer' and the 'seen' goes on. But it always remains 'the great and mysterious unknown'. One now sees the fact that the sense of 'I-am-ness' is in reality the sense of not-knowingness. Wanting to know is wanting to grab for one's own self-centred aims. Thus wanting to know invests the fact of 'not-knowingness' with a fictitious knowingness. And this knowingness, this experience, thereafter takes the place of 'pure seeing'. It is thereafter seeing through experiencing, with 'I-ness' as the experiencer. The *experiencer* thus usurps the place of the '*seer*'.

Why must this be so? This question contains the whole mystery of life as relatedness. *Asmita* confronted with this mystery becomes aware of *avidya* – unawareness of 'what is' in its totality. One sees that to interpose 'I-ness' in between the 'seer' and the 'seen' is to break the totality of 'what is', the totality of relatedness, into fragments, one fragment calling itself the observer or the experiencer, and the latter naming the other object or the observed, the experienced. In this manner the experiencer, *asmita*, is born of *avidya*, and later gets firmly entrenched in *abhinivesa*. The irrespressible sense of self-importance inevitably operates in the interest of self-perpetuation – which is the very nature of *abhinivesa*. One now sees why *avidya* makes man regard that as permanent which in fact is ephemeral; that as pure which in fact is impure; and that as pleasurable which in fact is painful. The tendency towards self-perpetuation naturally results in assuming that as permanent which subserves the ends of self-importance. The origin of the concept of the immortality and eternity of the personal self (*atma*) perhaps lies in this form of *avidya*. Again, the tendency towards self-justification and self-righteousness results in assuming that as pure which in fact is impure, and lastly, self-indulgence in what is felt as likeable results in assuming that as pleasurable which in fact is painful. *Avidya* ending up in *abhinivesa* thus turns upside down the whole world of reality. This is called *avidya-khyati* in Sutra 5.

It is only when one realizes that 'all is sorrow' (Sutra 15), that a new intelligence is born. Awareness or perception that 'all is sorrow' is *viveka* or existential intelligence. It is existential because it is this intelligence that enables man to distinguish between the tensions-born world-view and the world-view that is free of tensions. It is this intelligence that sets off a counter-movement, called *pratiprasava*. And it is this movement of counter-creation when it runs right through all tensions, beginning with *abhinivesa* and ending with *avidya*, that exposes to view the entire nature and structure of one's conditioned psyche.

Pratiprasava brings one the awareness of two central facts of one's being and living: (i) either one gets identified with *vrttis* (*vrtti-sarupya*) and gets entangled in a world of tensions from which there can be no escape through any egocentric activity; or (ii) one sees this fact and refuses to move with this self-procreative and self-importance-perpetuating movement, a movement of *prasava*. If one opts for 'no movement' as a result of seeing that 'all is sorrow', then an altogether new movement comes into being, a movement of *pratiprasava*, or counter-creativity. And we have seen how this latter movement of perception reveals the nature and structure of one's conditioned psyche, with all its formidable ramifications.

Pratiprasava eliminates tensions and tension-born movement of *becoming*. With tensions becoming inoperative, one sees *asmita* as a point of being with no magnitude, experiencing everything but accumulating nothing. It is free from known, the past, and knows only one thing, namely that 'I-am-ness is not-knowingness', and that it is a fact of one's *being*. In this state of being, devoid of becoming, it sees *avidya* as 'unawareness of what is' in its totality. To refuse to move with becoming is to remain with being. It is this refusal and rejection of becoming that brings one face to face with *avidya*, which is now seen as unawareness of 'what is' in its totality. It is this unawareness of totality that enters into man and makes him conscious of himself. This self-consciousness implies division between 'I' and 'not I', developing into a fragmentary view of the world – a totality. This totality now holds one's attention in its fullness. *Avidya* is thus transformed into a sense of wonder with the totality of not-knowingness, at one end, and the Great Unknown (the totality that is the whole world), at the other.

It is in this extraordinary *state of being* that Reality, which is a mysterious relatedness between the 'seer' and the 'seen', unfolds itself and reveals the nature of each of these two factors of existence as a whole. This is the subject-matter of the following Sutras.

4
The 'Seer' and the 'Seen'

SUTRAS 18 TO 25

18. *Prakāśakriyāsthitiśīlam bhūtendriyāt-makam bhogāpavargartham dṛśyaṁ*

The 'seen' is that which has three attributes of energy: (i) inertia; (ii) action; and (iii) illumination. These three attributes [three-fold energies] manifest themselves in organic and inorganic bodies. And the *raison d'être* of their existence is to offer man experiences and to liberate him through the right perception of them. [All this together constitutes the 'seen'–the objective world.]

19. *Viśeṣāviśeṣa liṅgamātrā-liṅgani guṇaparvāni*

All forms generated by the three-fold energies [*gunas*] of the 'seen' are either unique or not unique, and either with or without visible marks. These are their characteristics.

20. *Draṣṭā dṛśimātrah śuddho-pi pratyayānupaśyah*

The 'seer' is nothing but seeing energy; and although in himself pure, he tends to see through experiences.

21. *Tadartha eva dṛśyasyā-tmā*

The 'seen' exists only for the 'seer'.

22. *Kṛtarthaṁ prati naṣṭamapyanaṣṭaṁ tadanyasādhāraṇatyāt*

It vanishes when the purpose for which it exists is accomplished. But it goes on existing for those other 'seers' [who remain mixed up with common experiences].

23. *Svasvāmiśaktyoh svarūpopalabdh hetuh saṅyogah*

The *raison d'être* of contact [between the 'seer' and the 'seen'] is to enable the lord of the 'seen' ['seer'] to discover his identity.

24. *Tasya heturavidyā*

Avidya is the cause of contact [between the 'seer' and the 'seen'].

25. *Tadabhāvātsaṅyogābhāvo hānaṁ taddṛséh kaivalyaṁ*

The negation of *avidya* brings about the negation of contact. Abandonment of both is called the freedom of the 'seer'.

NOTES AND COMMENTS

These Sutras tell us how the 'seer' and the 'seen' disclose their existential nature to one who is free from tensions, and whose perception is illuminated by the emergence of existential intelligence (*viveka*).

We all know that we exist. And we also know that the world in which we find ourselves also exists. It is obvious that existence must necessarily be a manifestation of cosmic energy. To manifest is 'to reveal', 'to show plainly to the eye or the mind'. Energy 'revealing itself to the eye or the mind', is existence manifested as the world in which we live. There can be no existence without energy and there can be no affirmation or denial in respect of energy unless it reveals itself to the eye or the mind as the manifested world.

At the human level it is obvious that the cosmic energy that reveals itself to our eyes or mind as the world is as though polarized into two: the 'seer' and the 'seen'. Man assumes that he is the 'seer' and that what spreads before his eyes or mind is the world or the 'seen'. But when confronted with the question: what is the nature of the 'seer' and of the 'seen'? one is confused. For the discipline of Yoga, this is the question of all questions. There can be no real answer to any question unless three basic factors that always underlie any serious question are clearly understood. These three factors are: (i) the nature of the 'seen'; (ii) the nature of the 'seer'; and (iii) the nature of the existential relationship between the 'seer' and the 'seen'. Unless there is a clear understanding of each of these three factors which underlie any question about life or existence, nothing but confusion will reign supreme over human life.

The discipline of Yoga brings one face to face with this existential situation. At the very outset it drew our attention to the ideational choice-making movements of our mind, and helped us to see the truth that so long as we remain identified with *vrttis* there can be no perception of 'what is'. Perception of this truth brings one an intense awareness of the utmost importance of *vrtti-nirodha* for perception of 'what is,' that is, the nature of our existence in this world. And as one tries to remain in the state of *vrtti-nirodha* one encounters a number of impediments which prevent one from persisting in the state in which the mind remains devoid of *vrttis*. The Yoga Sutras then bring us face to face with the nature of these impediments and show us the necessity of action which enables one to abide in the state of Yoga.

This is called *Kriya Yoga*. This Yogic action reveals the fact that it is the operation of inner tensions (*klesas*) that generates impediments to one's abiding in the state of Yoga. The Sutras then expound the nature of these tensions and show us how they condition the human psyche. And they also show us the way of *pratiprasava* which eliminates all tensions. Through *pratiprasava*, one arrives at a stage in which one's mind is free of tensions and one's perception is illuminated by the emergence of existential intelligence (*viveka*). What does one see now? One sees clearly the existential nature of both the 'seen' and the 'seer'.

Sutra 18 describes the existential nature of the observable world, the 'seen'. Actually the very act of intelligent perception (*viveka*), delicately sensitive to everything within and without, reveals the nature of the objective world. One sees that one's psychosomatic organism is an integral part of the objective world. It is as though the entire objective world is compressed into our body, and manifests its nature through the operations that are going on there, from moment to moment. One becomes aware of the fact that 'what is here is everywhere; and what is not here is nowhere'. In this state one sees one's body in a state of rest and its activity is negligible. One identifies this state as inactive energy or inertia (*sthiti*). One then observes a variety of activities in one's body and mind which are as though charged with energy that is free from inertia. One identifies this 'energy in action' as *kriya*. And through the perception of *kriya* one becomes aware of the fact that the energy that helped us to identify inertia and action is by nature illuminational (*prakasa*). All this becomes possible because of 'choiceless awareness'.

The entire objective world (including one's body), is thus seen to be composed of the three-fold energies (*gunas*), named as *prakasa*, *kriya* and *sthiti*. As a modern man, one finds this description of the objective world amazing. At the physical level all objects are naturally found to be subject to inertia, which is resistance to change. And modern science tells us, as a result of careful observation and intelligent experiments, that all bodies in this world tend to remain in a state of rest, or in a state of uniform motion, until they are acted upon by forces external to them. This is the modern scientific law of inertia. At the physical level action comes from the uneven distribution of gravitational forces. At the biological level action comes from vital forces which charge inorganic matter with the energy of life. And at the psychological level, carrying the past with it, action comes from the ideational choice-making movements of the mind.

The whole of the objective world is thus seen to be a product of the natural interplay of the three-fold energies as described in Sutra 18. These three-fold energies (*gunas*) manifest themselves in inorganic objects (*bhutatmaka*) and organic objects (*indriyatmaka*). And this organic–inorganic world is experienced by man. The experiencing is self-illuminating energy.

It must be noted here that these three-fold energies of nature are integral. They cannot be separated from each other. But they can be distinguished, each one from the other two. When the aspect of inertia (*sthiti*) is dominant and the other two aspects are relatively dormant, we call such an object a physical body (*bhuta*). When the aspect of spontaneous action (*kriya*), that is, innate self-generating action, is dominant and the other two are dormant, we call that object an animate being, a living organism endowed with sensitivity (*indriyatmaka*). And when the aspects of self-illumination (*prakasa*) is dominant and the other two are dormant, we call that entity a self-conscious being. Man is perhaps the most pronouncedly self-conscious being in the animate world. Thus the uniting of the three-fold energies (*gunas*) of nature persist in all objects as an innate ecological balance of their mutual interactions. This balance varies in favour of one or the other of the three-fold energies. But it always remains integral. The whole objective world, along with its bewildering variety of animate and inanimate bodies, is thus held together in an ecological balance by the force of the innate and ever changing equilibrium of the three-fold energies of nature.

The question arises: what is all this for? To what end? The answer of Yoga is: *Bhogapavargartha. Bhoga* means experience; and *apavarga* means freedom through experiences. Man, on the one hand, and the world as a whole, on the other (including the human organism), become related to each other through sensuous experiences, and through nothing else. If there were no experiences, everything would remain obscure and utterly unintelligible. Therefore, experience (*bhoga*) is the existential link (*yoga*) between man and the world. It is thus clear that, so far as man at any rate is concerned, the world exists to offer *bhoga* or experiences to man. But man finds that experiences are conflicting; they generate tension, confusion and chaos, which threaten survival. Man, therefore, must, in the interests of survival, subject his experiences to careful observation and critical scrutiny with a view to finding a way out of tension, confusion and chaos.

Those who care to do so discover a way out, the way of *pratiprasava*, which leads to freedom from all tensions and tension-ridden conflict, confusion and chaos. Consequently, says Sutra 18, the existential *raison d'ětre* of the entire objective world (the 'seen'), is to offer experiences (*bhoga*) to man (the 'seer'), and liberate (*apayarga*) him through the right understanding of all experiences.

The expression *bhogapavartha* needs to be understood in the right way. It appears to make and in fact sounds like a teleological statement. But this is not so. Who can pretend to know the purpose or ultimate design of this mysterious universe? Yoga does not pretend to do so. All that this expression does is affirm the existential situation. It is a fact that man experiences only that which existence as a whole offers to him. The world does offer him experiences which may be painful, painless, or otherwise. To say, therefore, that the world exists to offer experiences to man is to state a bare fact of the existential situation. Secondly, it is also a fact that experiences are conflicting, that they generate tensions, confusion and chaos, which threaten the very existence of man on this earth. Man is thus forced, by the imperatives of existence itself, to find a way out. A way out means a way out of tensions, confusion, chaos and the threat to survival. That which enables man to do this is perception, a gift of existence itself to him. It is perception, a matter of choiceless awareness, that leads to the elimination of all those inner tensions which conflicting experiences inevitably generate. Therefore, to say that the objective world exists to offer experiences or *bhoga* to man, and, through right perception of *bhoga*, to liberate him from confusion, chaos and all threats to his survival (*apavarga*), is not to project a purpose or design on the world in the form of mental construct, but to state the very inherent implication of the existential situation. And this is precisely what the expression *bhogapavargartha* means and implies.

The word *bhoga* literally means 'eating, consuming, enjoyment, fruition'. Living beings must consume appropriate eatable objects in the world of nature in suitable quantities to survive. This is an existential imperative. This is *bhoga*. *Bhoga* is the existential link (*yoga*) between man and the world. *Bhoga* is thus experiencing of that which connects man to the world in the existential sense. And when man gets confronted with conflicting experiences, that is to say, when that which connects him to existence becomes confused and obscure, he is forced, by his very urge to survive, to look at his experiences with a view to finding a way out of confusion, conflict and chaos. This also is an existential imperative. This way out to freedom from *bhoga* is called *apavarga*.

The word *apa-varga* is a compound of *varga* with the prefix *apa*. *Apa* means 'away from'. The word *varga* is derived from the root *vrj* which means 'to choose'. It has other meanings also; but they are not relevant here. *Apavarga* therefore means 'a movement away from choosing'. *Bhoga* is invariably a product of the tendency to choose, which results in built-in likes and dislikes. The expression *bhogapavargartha*, thus means the objective, observable world (the 'seen') exists for offering experiences (*bhoga*) to man and, through *bhoga*, to liberate him from all tensions, confusion, conflict, and chaos – a movement generated by *bhoga*. *Apavarga* thus means a movement away from *bhoga*, away from the tendency to choose which results in *bhoga*.

Sutra 19 says that *drsya* or the 'seen' or the objects in the world, are either unique or non-unique, and either they have visible marks by which they can be identified or they are without such marks. This again is a statement of fact born of perception which has been liberated from tensions.

Sutra 20 describes the existential nature of the 'seer'. When the whole world, including the human organism, is a product of the three-fold energies of nature, what then remains for any description of the 'seer'? What remains is the 'energy of seeing' which enables man to perceive the existential nature of the observable world, the 'seen'. The 'observer' and the 'observed' imply and necessitate each other. But the observed, the 'seen', cannot be the 'seer' or the observer. The entire human organism is the observed, the 'seen'. If in this organism there were nothing else to make the world observable, existence as a whole would forever remain obscure and unintelligible. But the fact is that it is observable and intelligible. It becomes so through experiences, which the world offers to man. And when experiences confuse the mind, man has to find a way out. The way out is offered by pure perception, the energy of pure seeing (*drsimatra*). This energy naturally operates through experiences (*pratyaya*). And when experiences confuse the mind, the latter has to be freed from the ideational choice-making movements, which lie at the bottom of all confusion. The discipline of Yoga brings this about. The vision in a state of Yoga discloses that the entire observable world exists to liberate the 'seer' from his confused entanglement with the 'seen' (Sutra 21).

Sutra 22 is rather intriguing. It says that when the *raison d'être* of the objective world is accomplished by the liberation of by the 'seer' from his confusing entanglement with the 'seen', the world vanishes from his view. But it continues to operate for those other 'seers' who remain entangled in common experiences. If liberation means the destruction of the objective world for the 'seer', why does he continue to exist and what is the point of his being there at all? The point is that what actually vanishes is the world-view generated by *avidya*. This is the so-called objective world. In the view of man caught up in *avidya* and *avidya*-born tensions this is the so-called objective world. It is this confused, upside-down world, that vanishes from the view of the liberated 'seer'. He thereafter lives in a world of reality born of *viveka-khyati*. His way of living becomes Yogic, from moment to moment. This Yogic way of living is described in the Sutras that follow. And its culmination or perfection is described in the very last Sutra of the last Part.

Sutras 23 to 25 explain that those caught up in *avidya-khyati* remain in a world of make-believe, whether they be very learned, as mentioned in Sutra 9 which deals with *abhinivesa*, or whether they be very ignorant. They remain caught up in a world of illusion because they fail to see that *sanyoga* (contact between the 'seer' and the 'seen') is existentially meant to help them to discover their existential identity (Sutra 23). They also fail to see the fact that *avidya* is the efficient cause of *sanyoga* (Sutra 24). But one who sees the existential significance of *sanyoga* and *avidya*, at once opts for *Kriya Yoga*, negates *avidya* and finds that *sanyoga* is no longer there. The world-view born of *avidya* and *sanyoga* disappears into nothingness. The 'seer' thereafter gets established in his existential identity and lives in total freedom (*kaivalya*), as stated in Sutra 25.

The Sutras that follow describe the characteristics of the Yogic way of living that is born of freedom, abides in freedom and flowers into ever new creation (IV-34).

5
The Eight-Petalled Flower of Yoga (1)

SUTRAS 26 TO 29

26. *Viveka-khyātiraviplavā hānopāyah*
Vision born of discerning intelligence, which is free from drifting about in different directions, is the way to negate [the confusion caused by *avidya*].

27. *Tasya saptadhā prāntabhūmih prajñā*
Wisdom born of discerning intelligence, which is the way to negate, extends up to the seven regions [of the eight-fold Yogic way of living].

28. *Yogāṅgānuṣṭhānādaśuddhi-kṣaye jñanadīptirā viveka-khyātih*
When the impurities are eliminated by the adoption of the eight-fold way of Yoga, the vision of the discerning intelligence acquires extraordinary brilliance.

29. *Yama-niyamā-sana-prāṇāyāma-pratyāhāra-dhāraṇā-dhyāna-samādhayo-ṣṭāvaṅgāni*
Yama, *niyama*, *asana*, *pranayama*, *pratyahara*, *dharana*, *dhyana* and *Samadhi* are the eight aspects of Yoga [the Yogic way of living].

NOTES AND COMMENTS

With the emergence of *viveka* (Sutra 15), or discerning intelligence, an altogether new style of life comes into being, which is called the Yogic way of living (*Yoganganusthana*, Sutra 28). *Viveka-khyati* (Sutra 26) means vision or a world-view (*khyati*) born of *viveka* or discerning intelligence (Sutra 15). Men are born and brought up in *avidya-khyati* which is the inherent characteristic of the evolutionary flow of nature (*prakrtyapura*, IV-2). Therefore, their whole way of living is determined or conditioned by *avidya-khyati*. *Avidya-khyati* is a vision or a world-view in which one is unable to distinguish the *real* from the *ideational*, the factual from the wishful. The two get mixed up and so confusion reigns supreme over human life. Because of this confusion one assumes that as permanent which in fact is ephemeral; that as pure which in fact is impure; and that as pleasurable which in fact is painful (Sutra 5). *Avidya-khyati* is thus an upside-down world-view in which there is total distortion of reality that is, of the existential situation.

When this world-view leads man to unending sorrow, he begins to question this traditional or conformist world-view born of conditioned consciousness. It is this questioning which gives birth to discerning intelligence (*viveka*). And when one begins to live in the light of this existential intelligence, one's new way of living unfolds into eight aspects of life as an integral whole. This is called *astanga-Yoga* or the eight-fold Yogic way of living. These eight aspects of the Yogic way of living are ennumerated in Sutra 39. And in the following Sutras the significance of each of these eight aspects is briefly but precisely explained.

In the view of Yoga, man must either opt for the Yogic way of living, or remain in *avidya-khyati*, which will inevitably land him repeatedly in unending sorrow and misery and continue to entangle him in tensions, confusion, conflict and chaos – all of which develop into a threat to his very survival on this planet. Therefore, man must either adopt a Yogic way of living or become extinct as many species have become extinct in the past, as a result of a failure to adapt to the ever-changing existential situation.

The eight-fold Yogic way of living is a way that brings about a radical transformation in the mind of the man who is dominated by *avidya-khyati*. In the absence of such a radical transformation, man must continue to be dominated by a world-view born of *avidya-khyati*. Whatever the marvellous looking facets of this historical, traditional and conformist world-view – secular or religious, physical or metaphysical, scientific or ideological, temporal or transcendental – none of them can ever enable man to establish a vital and meaningful rapport with the existential situation. Occasionally and erratically, men dominated by such a world-view (born of *avidya-khyati*), may come upon some factual discoveries in this or that field of life. But any world-view founded on such disjoined and disconnected discoveries must necessarily remain fragmentary and, as such, must necessarily result in tensions, confusion, conflict and chaos which generate an ever-mounting threat to human survival. And this remains so even to this day.

Therefore, the ever-changing existential situation demands a radical transformation in the mind itself, and not in merely in some of the aspects of the world-view born of *avidya-khyati*. Changes in this or that aspect must necessarily remain fragmentary; they can never touch the core of the matter. This core is the quality of the mind. And therefore if transformation is to be real and radical it must take place at this central core. Peripheral changes have taken place throughout the long history of man. But they have left the central point of the existential human situation wholly untouched. Tensions, confusion, conflict and ever-mounting chaos continue even today to threaten man and life. It is only the Yogic 'seers', in the sense of the Yoga Sutras, who saw where and how the radical change must occur to take man out of his suicidal or murderous predicament.

Sutra 26 says that *viveka-khyati* is the way out of this predicament. It enables man to reject the whole structure of the mind born of *avidya-khyati*, and thus creates conditions necessary for its total transformation. It is capable of doing so because it comes into being as a result of seeing the mischief that *avidya* does to man's mind. Consequently it becomes free of tensions by the very fact of the rejection of *avidya-khyati*. It is like seeing a poisonous snake and stepping out of its way. The threat to the survival of man as a decent human being which *avidya-khyati* generates is infinitely more devastating than the one which a snake presents. A snake may kill an individual, whereas the threat which *avidya-khyati* generates has been swallowing countless generations of mankind for countless centuries. The very perception of this horror imparts to *viveka-khyati* a quality which eliminates tensions and makes it *aviplava*.

Viplava means 'drifting about, floating in different directions'. *Viplava* is that which generates chaos in man's mind and thus forces him to run helter-skelter in utter darkness in search of fulfilment of his senseless and chaotic wants. *Viveka-khyati* puts an end to the darkness generated by *viplava* by the very light of discerning intelligence which emerges out of the perception that 'all is sorrow' (Sutra 15).

Sutra 28 says that the light of *viveka-khyati* extends as far as the first seven aspects of the eight-fold Yogic way of living mentioned in Sutra 29. It is only the last aspect, namely *Samadhi*, which remains beyond the range of *viveka-khyati*. This is so because *Samadhi* is a kind of mutational explosion for which *viveka-khyati* creates the necessary conditions. This explosion transcends *viveka-khyati*. As one lives his daily life in the light of *viveka-khyati*, the mystery that is life begins to unfold itself. Like a bud unfolding its petals, life unfolds itself petal by petal, establishing one more and more vitally and deeply in the very heart of life. This procession is an eternal cosmic wonder. In this process, as Sutra 28 says, with the unfolding of each petal one's psychosomatic organism casts away its impurities. And, as it becomes more and more pure in its perception and action, *viveka-khyati* acquires extraordinary brilliance, illuminating almost the whole range of human life and its existential relationship with the objective world (Sutra 28).

Sutra 29 enumerates the eight aspects of the Yogic way of life. Each of these aspects is explained in Sutras 30 to 55 of Part II, and in Sutras 1 to 3 of Part III. Most of these Sutras speak for themselves. But it will be necessary to probe into this 'Eight-petalled flower of Yoga' with a view to grasping its immense significance for human life. We shall therefore add a few comments on the Eight-petalled flower of Yoga in the next chapter.

SUTRAS 30 TO 55

30. *Ahiṁsā-satyāsteya-brahmacaryā-parigraha yamāh*

Non-violence, truth, non-stealing, austerity of learning and non-accumulation – these five are called *yamas.*

31. *Jati-deśa-kāla-samayānavaccinnah sārvabhaumā mahāvrataṁ*

These (*yamas*) together constitute the greatest vow of austere observance, inasmuch as they are basic and cover the entire field of life and existence and as such remain unaffected and unbound by the limitations of birth, country or place, time and circumstance.

32. *Śouca-saṅtoṣa-tapah svādhyāye-ṣvara-praṇidhānāni niyamāh*

Purity, quiet contentment, austerity, self-study and meditation of God – these five are called *niyamas.*

33. *Vitarkabādhane pratipakṣa-bhāvanaṁ*

In the event of harassing argumentation, meditation to counter its effects is suggested.

34. *Vitarkā hiṁsādayāh Krtạkāritānumoditā lobhakṛodhamoha-pūrvakā mṛdumadhyādhimātrā dukkhājñānānaṅtaphalā iti prati-pakṣa-bhāvanaṁ*

Harassing argumentations [*vitarkas*] take five forms, namely violence, untruthfulness, stealing, non-austerity in learning, and accumulation [the opposites of the five *yamas*]. These are brought about by our own actions, or by the actions of others which have been provoked by us, or by our approval of those actions. These are motivated by greed, anger and insensibility at low, medium or high level. And they result in an endless progeny of misery and ignorance. The awareness of this whole process is called *pratipaksabhavanam* [meditation to counter involvement in argument].

35. *Ahiṁsāpratiṣṭhāyāṁ tatsannidhou vairatyāgah*

When one gets firmly established in non-violence, an atmosphere of non-hostility prevails in one's vicinity, which induces others to discard hostility.

36. *Satyapratiṣṭhāyāṁ Kriyāphalā- ṣrayatvaṁ*

When one gets firmly established in truth, it operates as a ground for the fruition of action.

37. *Asteyapratiṣṭhāyām sarvaratnopasthānaṁ*

When one is firmly established in non-stealing all varieties of precious stones become available in one's vicinity.

38. *Brahmacarya- pratiṣṭhāyām vīrya-lābhah*

When one is firmly established in the austerity of learning one acquires extraordinary energy.

39. *Aparigrahasthairye janmakathaṅtāsaṁbodhah*

When one is firmly established in non-accumulation, one understands how one's present life has come to be what it is.

40. *Śoucātsvāṅgajugupsa parairasaṅsargah*

Observance of purity brings about aversion to one's bodily urges and a disinclination to touch any other body.

41. *Satvaśuddhisoumanansyaikāgryeṅdriya-jayātmadarśana-yogyatvāni ca*

It also brings about purification of life, kindheartedness, one-pointedness, mastery over the senses and the ability to understand oneself.

42. *Santoṣādanuttamah sukhalābhah*

Quiet contentment brings about a sense of extraordinary happiness.

43. *Kayeṅdriyasiddhiraśuddhikṣayāttapasah*

Austerity brings about mastery over the body and the senses through the elimination of impurities.

44. *Svādhyāyādiṣṭadevatāsaṁprayogah*

Self-study brings about an atmosphere conducive to the presence of divine powers beneficial to one's being.

45. *Samādhisiddhirīṣvarapraṇidhanat*

Meditational awareness of God brings about the attainment of *Samadhi.*

46. *Sthirasukhamāsanaṁ*

A body-posture that results in a steady state of comfort is called *asana*.

47. *Prayatnaśaithilyānanta-samāpattibhyām*

Such a posture [*asana*] comes about through total relaxation of effort and through a state of mind in harmony with the infinite state of repose.

48. *Tato dvaṅdvānabhighātah*

Establishment in *asana* brings about a state of being in which one remains unaffected by the pairs of opposites.

49. *Tasminsati ṣvāsapraṣvāsayoragativicchedah prāṇāyāmah*

While established in *asana*, the break in the continuance of incoming and outgoing breath is called *pranayama*.

50. *Bāhyābhyaṅtarastambha-vṛttirdeśakālasaṅkhyābhih paridṛṣṭo dīrghasūkṣmah*

It [*pranayama*] is a stillness consequent on a break in the continuity which comes at the end of the incoming and outgoing breath. It is found to have measurable length in space and time-duration; and it becomes prolonged and subtle.

51. *Bāhyābhyaṅtaraviṣạyākṣepī caturthah*

Pranayama which discards its three forms [mentioned in the above Sutra] is the fourth form.

52. *Tatah kṣīyate prakāśāvaranaṁ*

Thereby the veils which cover self-illumination are removed.

53. *Dhāraṇāsu ca yogyatā manasah*

It also helps one's mind to acquire the necessary capacity for *dharana*.

54. *Svaviṣayāsaṁprayoge cittasvarūpānukāra iveṅdriyāṇām pratyāhārah*

When the senses cease to move towards their respective objects, and merge as it were in the existential quality of the mind in itself, such a state is called *pratyahara*.

55. *Tatah paramāvaśyateṅdriyāṇām*

Through *pratyahara* a total mastery over the senses is attained.

NOTE

Sutras 30 to 55 cover the five aspects (*angas*) of the Yogic way of living. The last three aspects are explained in Sutras 1 to 3 of Part III.

PART THREE
Vibhuti pada

1
The Eight-Petalled Flower of Yoga (2)

SUTRAS 1 TO 3

1. *Deśabandhaścittasya dhāraṇā*
The mind held within the emptiness of space is called *dharana.*
2. *Tatra pratyaikatānatā dhyānaṁ*
There [in *dharana*] the in-tuneness with the single act of experiencing is called *dhyana.*
3. *Tadevarthamātra nirbhasam svarūpaśūnyamiva Samādhih*
That alone which radiates the splendour of objectivity in its purity and in which one's identity is reduced as it were to utter emptiness, is called *Samadhi.*

NOTES AND COMMENTS

These eight aspects of Yoga (II-29) together constitute the eight-fold Yogic way of living. It is a way in which an age-old, slumbering mind awakens into a radiant clarity of vision. It brings about a radical and total transformation of the mind which until now has been caught in the darkness of *avidya-khyati*, into the radiance of *viveka-khyati*. It is the passage of man from the darkness of the *natural* state to the illumination of a *cultural* state. It is a mutational transformation of the world-view born of *avidya*, or unawareness of 'what is', into the world-view born of *viveka*, or discerning intelligence which illuminates 'what is' with the existential splendour of pure objectivity. It is a radical transformation of the nature-made man into a Yoga-made authentic human being in harmony with existence as a whole.

Let us now see what happens when one rejects the world-view born of *avidya-khyati* and turns towards the world-view illuminated by *viveka-khyati*.

The first thing that happens, as pointed out in Sutra 26 of Part II, is that the mind that was previously floating about in different directions in a chaotic manner now ceases to move in any direction. It sees that all was disorder while one was held a captive by *avidya-khyati*. That disorder is a threat to human survival. As one looks at the nature and structure of the disorder in which one was caught up, and within the confines of which one was striving hard to bring order through the ideational choice-making tendency of the mind a new vision of a real, existential order begins to unfold itself. One sees how ideation generates a false world-view and thus one realizes that all ideation must cease for the existential to be seen and understood. This realization unfolds the motivating factors that bring disorder into man's life. These factors are born of greed (*lobha*), anger (*krodha*) and insensibility (*moha*) which have their roots in egocentricity. This operates at all levels of one's blindly accepted traditional and temporal way of living. It is because of this that one tends towards violence, falsehood, stealing, an easy-going way of living in utter disregard of learning, and the accumulation of goods, material and mental, that give sustenance to such a way of living. One goes on living in this egocentric manner so long as it works. This way of living goes on until one finds oneself face to face with a situation which reveals that whatever one may think feel or do, it must necessarily result in unending sorrow and unlimited misery. One is now face to face with a total disorder which threatens one's survial. This perception reveals that all that survival demands is an awareness of 'need' to the total exclusion of 'greed'. The needs of survival have natural limits. Food, clothing, shelter and sex – all have natural limitations. It is only when one crosses the line of natural limitations, and thus turns natural needs into monstrous greeds, that all the trouble starts and generates ever expanding disorder. It is this expanding disorder that develops into an ever mounting threat to survival (II-34).

Viveka, or discerning intelligence, thus uncovers the nature and structure of the *avidya*-born way of living. One now sees with radiant clarity that there can be no order and survival for man unless he sees the urgency of a way of living in which no corner is given to violence, falsehood, stealing, disregard of learning, and greedy accumulation. These five constitute what are called *yamas*, or existential imperatives. They mean and imply that one cannot allow oneself to be violent, directly or indirectly, and at the same time hope to see the reality of the existential situation. The same is true of the other four *yamas*. One cannot go on being false to oneself, one cannot go on stealing, one cannot go on ignoring the importance of learning about life which demands austerity, and one cannot go on accumulating material goods and mental preferences to the detriment of one's identity and at the cost of one's fellow human beings, and at the same time hope to sees the reality of the existential situation. Therefore, non-violence, truth, non-stealing, austerity of learning, and non-accumulation are existential imperatives, the observance of which must be regarded as an uncompromising vow, irrespective of one's birth, the times in which one lives and the circumstances which one may have to face. The limitations of birth, time or circumstance must never be allowed to compromise any of the five existential imperatives or *yamas* (Sutra 31). This is possible if one sees clearly the absolute importance of these *yamas* as necessary pre-conditions for the right understanding of the existential situation in which man finds himself. They are not ideas or ideals to be followed half-heartedly. They are hard, rock-bottom facts which must be seen and understood. It is this razor-sharp precision of understanding that of itself will make these *yamas* integral parts of one's being and living. No egocentric effort will then be necessary in order to bear them constantly in mind. They will be as natural and effortless as one's breathing for which no egocentric effort or practice is called for. The very perception of the self-perpetuating horror that the opposites of the *yamas* bring into human life, as stated in Sutra 34, will would make one naturally alert, attentive and watchful about getting involved in them. And if, despite one's watchfulness, any of these opposites appear in one's mind, the way to combat them is described in Sutra 33. This is a way of meditation which is self-illuminating and which disperses all shadows cast by any kind of confused thinking born of the past-driven *vrttis* of conditioned consciousness.

Sutra 32 enumerates the five *niyamas*, which, along with *yamas*, form an integral aspect of the eight-fold Yogic way of living. Of these five *niyamas*, three – *tapa, svadhyaya* and *isvarapranidhana* – have already been explained in our comments on Sutra 1 of Part II. Together they constitute *Kriya Yoga*, or Yoga in action in one's day-to-day living. The remaining two needs some clarification.

Soucha means purification of one's psychosomatic organism. The way of Yoga demands purification in the same way as the extraction of pure gold demands purification of gold-bearing clods of dirt. Body and mind-stuff are the products of the evolutionary and social and historical past. The gold of pure perception that gets mixed up with them through contact born of *avidya*, has to be separated from the accumulated refuge of the past. The process of this separation starts, not at the physical but at the psychological and perceptive level. It is a process of *Kriya Yoga*, *pratiprasava* and *viveka-khyati*, expounded in Part II. It is actually a process of distinguishing between the 'seer' and the 'seen' through the discerning intelligence. Once this distinction forms an integral part of one's being and daily living, the discipline of Yoga then acquires a self-correcting and self-propagating movement in harmony with the unseen operation of existence as a whole.

Soucha or self-purification thus becomes an integral part of *astanga-yoga*, the eight-fold way. This purification naturally follows 'pure seeing', which has to be disentangled from seeing through the coloured lenses of past experiences. This disentanglement is the very core of purification. It brings about a sense of sacredness in regard to all forms of life, including one's own psychosomatic organization. And since contact (*sanyoga*) caused by *avidya* lies at the bottom of all forms of impurity and corruption, at all levels of one's being and living, one's disentanglement from contact, including the contact with one's body-based consciousness, becomes the necessary prerequisite for purification. The violation and exploitation of one's body and mind for egocentric ends must therefore end for purification to be.

Santosa or quiet contentment is also a prerequisite which forms part of *niyama*. Once the past-driven momentum of egocentric ends and wants slows down, quiet contentment naturally comes into being. Desire, craving, greed and unquenchable hunger or thirst (*trsna*) for more and more of everything thought to be desirable, lose their drive, and the mind then naturally takes repose in quiet contentment. Nothing thereafter matters except that which promotes pure seeing and right understanding of the existential situation.

It is necessary to note the distinction between *yamas* and *niyamas*. The former are existential imperatives, whereas the latter are man-made decisions and actions that follow perception of the necessity for the discipline of Yoga.

Sutras 35 to 45 explain what naturally happens when one is established in *yama* and *niyama*, the two basic prerequisites of the eight-fold way. They create the necessary conditions at the intellectual and emotional levels for the unfolding of the other petals of the eight-petalled flower of Yoga.

Asana, or posture, is the third petal, or aspect, of *astanga-yoga*. One established in *yama* and *niyama* as it were looks at his body with a new sense of wonder as though it were a mystery. An infinite number of subtle and gross activities are always going on in one's body. How and why they go on remains an eternal mystery. Explanations by biologists, physiologists, psychologists, and scientists dealing with the physico-chemical constituents of animal and human organisms, may throw some light one some of their operations and pretend to offer solutions to some of the problems generated by man's stupid exploitation of his wondrous organism. But all such explanations and so-called solutions must necessarily be the products of fragmentary approaches to the existential situation. As such they do more harm than good. Besides this they generate false hopes for the future.

Yoga discards all such fragmentary approaches to the existential situation. They all belong to the domain of a world-view born of *avidya-khyati*. Yoga, therefore, first and foremost, attacks *avidya-khyati* and negates it by *viveka-khyati*. It is this basic and integral approach that leads to the emergence of the Yogic eight-fold way of living. It is with the eyes of this integral approach that one looks at one's body and discovers that when the body is in the right posture this brings about an existential rapport with the world in which one finds one's being. It is now with the clear comprehension of *yama* and *niyama* that one looks at one's body and its movements, gross or subtle. This very look enables one to discover, after some trial and error, a posture which has immense significance. One sees the necessity of total relaxation of all effort (Sutra 47), and of letting the body find its own natural angle of repose. One sees that all effort is egocentric and, therefore, capable of infinite mischief. As one discards effort and relaxes, one discovers a posture in which one can stay with steady comfort without being bothered by time or impatience. In this Yogic posture (*asana*) one finds oneself in a state of mind in harmony with the state of repose which is endless (Sutra 47). It is as though a cosmic 'angle of repose' in which inertia (*sthiti*), and integral constituent of the three-fold energies of nature, becomes aware of itself. Inertia, as it were, gets illumined by 'pure seeing'. Cosmic inertia and one's bodily inertia coexist on the same wavelength. The body is in harmony with the world around at the inertial level, a harmony which is charged with the energy of 'pure seeing'.

One who finds himself in such a Yogic posture discovers that variations in temperature, within and without, heat and cold, and other pairs of opposites, leave the body unaffected (Sutra 48). This is a matter of experiment and experience in the Yogic way.

It needs to be noted here that the so-called Yogic *asanas* of various kinds, popularized by so-called Yogis, have no place whatsoever in the Yoga Sutras. They are all deviations from the path of Yoga as expounded in Patanjali's Yoga Sutras. These various types of *asanas* may have some therapeutic value for certain ailments, but they have no significance for Yoga as it is expounded in these Sutras.

Sutras 49 to 53 deal with *pranayama*, the fourth integral aspect of *astang-yoga*.

While one is well established in *asana*, one naturally observes that just as one's body in a steady state discloses the essence of the inertial principle (*sthiti*) of the three-fold energies of nature, the rhythm of breathing, that naturally goes on in the body at all times, discloses the essence of the active principle (*kriya*) of those three-fold energies. This is action in the existential sense, as opposed to activities triggered by the ideational movements of the mind. Actually, these latter are not properly speaking actions but reactions to the existential situation. Action, in the existential or the Yogic sense, is action that follows pure perception of 'what is'. Any time-lag between such perception and action is the result of *avidya* and *avidya*-born activities.

Pranayama is the discovery of a break (*vicheda*) in the continuity of the incoming and outgoing breath. Just as *vrtti-nirodha* is a break in the continuity of ideation, so *pranayama* is a break in the continuity of breathing. Again, just as energetic interest in the void devoid of *vritts* is *abhyasa* (I-13), so energetic interest in the break in the continuity of the breathing movement is *pranayama* (II-49). This energetic interest discloses four varieties of *pranayama*: (i) the break at the end of the outgoing breath; (ii) the break at the end of the incoming breath; (iii) the time-duration and length of space covered by the outgoing breath which discloses the prolongation and the subtleness of the void during the breaks, and (iv) the void during the break in which one loses all interest in measurements and the objects served by such measurements (Sutras 50 and 51).

Sutras 52 and 53 speak of what happens as a result of *pranayama*. Two things happen: (i) the realization of the existential nature of *kriya*, or the action-principle of the three-fold energies of nature, is seen to remove the coverings on the mind which came on it through temporal conditionings; and as a result, (ii) the emergence of a quality of mind necessary for *dharana*, which is explained in Sutra 1 of Part III.

It is pertinent to note here that the eight-fold Yoga brings about a pure perception of the existential nature of *sthiti, kriya* and *prakasa* which are the three-fold energies underlying the whole observable world of nature (Sutra 18). The interplay of these three-fold energies of nature results in the manifestation of the objective world. To perceive and realize this is to be aware of 'what is' or of the existential situation.

Sutras 54 and 55 deal with the fifth aspect of the *astanga-yoga* (the eight-fold yoga, Sutra 29), namely, *pratyahara. Pratyahara* is a state of mind and of the entire psychosomatic organism, in which the natural, past-driven tendency of the senses to move towards their respective objects gets arrested and the senses as it were find their repose in the mind in its quietude. This quietude is in fact the existential nature of the mind (Sutra 54). Sutra 55 tells us that when this happens one naturally acquires a mastery over the senses. This mastery comes about because one sees how and why the senses keep moving towards their respective objects. They do so to offer experiences (*bhoga*) of the objective world to the 'seer'; and when one fully realizes the *raison d'être* of *bhoga*, one moves away from the hunger or thirst for more and more experiences and gets interested in *apavarga* (II-18).

Sutra 1 of this Part III describes the sixth aspect of the *astanga-yoga* which is called *dharana. Pranayama* and *pratyahara* together create conditions necessary for this extraordinary state, called *dharana*. It is a state in which *sthiti* and *kriya*, the two constituents of the three-fold energies of the objective word, including one's psychosomatic organism, are so slowed down that almost all the temporal coverings over the mind are removed and the third constituent, namely, *prakasa*, now dominates the whole scene. In the radiance of this *prakasa*, the mind gets emptied of all objects and is held within the confines of inner space. Man sees objects only when his senses are operative. But when they cease to be operative and their tendency to move towards their respective objects gets arrested as a result of *pratyahara*, the objective world, as it were, gets emptied of all sensuous objects. And even if objects are seen, they cease to attract the mind, which is now wholly interested in discovering the reality underlying the objective world. There is now emptiness within and emptiness without. This mind is held in this vast space (*desa*), as though it had been created in order to have this single experience of emptiness an emptiness devoid not only of *vrttis* but also of the objects (*drsya*) with which they tend to get identified – an emptiness which is full of immense significance, as though it was the very womb of reality.

In-tuneness with this single act experiencing of the pure emptiness of space is called *dhyana* (Sutra 2). When all other experiences merge in one experience of the total emptiness of space, time comes to a halt. Temporal movement is signified by a succession of experiences, coming one after the other. When this succession gets dissolved in one, single experience of empty space, within and without, time must necessarily come to a stop. This extraordinary state of pure experiencing without particular experiences is called *dhyana* or meditation.

And when one is established in *dhyana*, a pure experiencing without the experiencer, that is to say when one's identity loses all magnitude, or any identifiable mark or attribute, the objective world as it were, explodes into a radiant objectivity in its existential authenticity. This is *Samadhi* (Sutra 3)

One who goes through this wondrous process of the eight-fold way of Yogic living becomes an authentic human being who sees the world as it is in its existential purity. Such a one gets established in his existential identity in which pure seeing and real action go together. Such perceptual action is creation. It is capable of radically transforming the dark forces of nature into self-illumined energies of creation in total freedom.

2
From Samadhi to Sanyama

SUTRA 4 TO 8

4. *Trayamekatra Saṁyamah*

These three [*dharana-dhyana-Samadhi*] together are called *Sanyama.*

5. *Tajjayāt prajñālokah*

Mastery over *Sanyama* explodes into a resplendent world-view charged with wisdom.

6. *Tasya bhūmiṣu viniyogah*

It gets directed spontaneously to the various fields of life.

7. *Trayamaṁtaraṅgaṁ pūrvebhyah*

These three [*dharana-dhyana-Samadhi*] constitute the inner core of the first five [*yama*, *niyama*, *asana*, *pranayama* and *pratyahara*].

8. *Tadapi bahiraṅgaṁ nirbījasya*

And even the combination of these three is the external aspect of the seedless *Samadhi* ['stateless State'].

NOTES AND COMMENTS

These Sutras describe what happens when one has adopted and assimilated the eight-fold Yogic way of living.

Such a man, now become a Yogi, discovers that life, or the world, has two sides: the *external* and the *internal.* And although the eight-fold way of living is integral, in the sense that none of its eight aspects can be separated from the other seven, it also has two sides: external and internal. The first five aspects constitute the external side, and the last three constitute the inner core of this external side. It is like a bud sprouting into an eight-petalled flower, of which five petals form the exterior, while the other three form its inner core. And again, the Yogi further discovers that even this trinity of *dharana-dhyana-Samadhi* is the exterior of the innermost core, which is the seedless *Samadhi* – a '*stateless State*'.

The Yogi is a man who has undergone a radical transformation which enables him to see and discover what a non-Yogi can never do. A non-Yogi also has eyes to see, but his seeing is covered up and conditioned by *avidya-khyati.* The Yogi, on the other hand, is one who has walked out of the dark prison-house of *avidya-khyati*, and who has, by this revolutionary action come upon the luminous kingdom of *viveka-khyati.* His vision is now free of all conditionings. And his world-view is illuminated by resplendent wisdom.

From here onwards one is confronted with a different world, a world of reality of an altogether different dimension from the world in which men are born and brought up. Right from his birth, man is told about the world in which he finds himself. A verbal description of the world is dinned into his ears and mind, which he must accept on pain of being dragooned into being a docile social conformist. One who resists this pressure and refuses to conform is regarded as abnormal, a freak, or a mentally deranged person, a case of psychosis – a non-man, or a non-member of human society.

Man thus lives in a world of words – a verbal description which he tends to equate with reality. Words usurp the place of reality, the objective world. Man thus makes his acquaintance with the world through words. And he becomes so familiar with this mind-made world that anything beyond it, or outside its closed frontiers, is assumed by him to be unreal or illusive. It is like being introduced to a stranger by giving the name by which the stranger is known, the name of the family, the caste, the class, the place, the country, the religion or the creed to which he belongs; thereafter, the stranger becomes a known person, along with his verbal personal history. Whether it be an inanimate object like a river or a mountain, or an animate being like a dog, a cat, a fish in water, or a bird with wings, or a human being – in all these it is a name, a word, a verbal description that determines the nature and structure of human knowledge. And the development of knowledge turns out to be a development of a mere rhetoric – reactionary, reformist or revolutionary. Caught in this trap, man forgets that the word is not the thing, the description is not the described. And therein lies all the trouble to which man has become the bait.

Yoga demolishes this world, which is a mere description. It uproots man from his animal and social heritage, and brings him face to face with the reality that breathes in him, the reality that relates him vitally, existentially to the world of which he becomes conscious through his senses. Yoga does this without the medium of words, and of experiences that are dominated by word-generated knowledge and devoid of substance or reality.

Therefore, one who still lingers in the world of words – which is a mere description – will feel what is described in these and the following Sutras to be fantastic and unreal. And there is no way of convincing a word-oriented man of the real world, unless he happens to see the fact that the word is not the thing and that it can never relate him to a world of reality.

But one who opts for not choosing, and therefore for not-doing, *undoes* the familiar world. He then finds that the world of words, the world of doing, crumbles before his very eyes; and a new world, charged with resplendent reality begins to emerge out of darkness.

It is true that the Sutras, in expounding this new world of reality, also use words. But these words are like the finger that points at a faintly flickering star to help one to look in the right direction so that he may see it for himself and become convinced of its existence. Just as the finger pointing out a direction is not the star so also the words of the Sutras expounding the world of reality are not reality itself. They are used as mere pointers. Not words, but seeing in the direction to which the words point out, is what matters here.

Sutras 5 and 6 speak of how the Yogi deals with the objective world through a world-view charged with resplendent wisdom. This wisdom emerges out of the depth of one's being when one looks at the world through the eyes of *Sanyama* (Sutra 4). It is the coming into being of these new eyes which discloses to the Yogi that his body, a psychosomatic organism, is an entity which functions externally as though oriented by *yama, niyama, asana, pranayama* and *pratyahara*; and that these five external aspects of his being and living are luminously activated from within by the trinity of *dharana-dhyana-Samadhi*. He looks at the world through the eyes of this trinity which is called *Sanyama*. The *Astanga-Yoga* transforms the entire psychosomatic organism of the Yogi, which now operates as an integral whole, and not in a fragmentary manner as before. The trinity of *dharana-dhyana-Samadhi* (*Sanyama*) shines through his eyes and his organism acts in accordance with the new vision, a new world-view born of resplendent wisdom (*prajnaloka*, Sutra 5)

What the Yogi now sees and discovers is described in the following Sutras.

SUTRAS 9 TO 13

9. *Vyutthāna-nirodha-sanskārayorabhi-bhāva-prādurbhāvou nirodha-kṣana-chittānvayo nirodha-parināmah*

During the oscillation of the mind between the impressions of great activity and the impressions of non-activity or stillness, when the mind becomes associated with stillness, a transformation takes place which is called *nirodha-parinama*–a transformation brought about by association with a state devoid of movement.

10. *Tasya praśānta-vāhitā sanskārāt*

This transformation produces a flow of quietude through the force of repeated impressions of *nirodha* [non-movement].

11. *Sarvārthataikāgratayoh Kṣayodayou cittasya samādhi-parināmah*

The ending of the scattering away of the mind through its association with all kinds of objects, and its awakening into an all-inclusive one-pointedness, results in another transformation called *samadhi-parinama* [transformation stabilizing into *Samadhi*].

12. *Tatah punah śāntoditvu tulya-pratyayau cittasyaikāgratā-pariṇāmah*

These again, the balancing of the experience of quietude and that of the arising of all-inclusive one-pointedness, result in yet another transformation of the mind called *ekagrata-parinama* [transformation into an all-inclusive one-pointedness].

13. *Ettena bhūtendriyeṣu dharma-lakṣaṇāvasthā-pariṇāma vyākhyātah*

In this way, the three transformations of the body and the senses, namely, *dharma*, *laksana* and *avastha*, are also explained by the foregoing exposition [of the three transformations of the mind].

NOTES AND COMMENTS

As has been already pointed out, these Sutras expound the transformations which result from the application of *Sanyama* (Sutras 4, 5, 6) to the world within and without. In the first place the Yogi discovers that the first five aspects of *astanga-yoga* form the exterior of his being and living and the last three aspects form the interior; and that these three also form the exterior of the seedless *Samadhi*, the stateless state, which lies at the innermost core of his being.

Having thus discovered the existential nature and structure of his being, the Yogi now looks at the world around and discovers that as he looks at anything with the eyes of *Sanyama* (Sutra 4), three transformations take place in it one after the other.

Sutra 9 describes the first transformation. To understand the significance of this transformation one has to recollect that when one reaches the stage of *Samadhi* (Sutra 3), one realizes that what he calls his identity (*svarupa*) is an entity without any attribute; it is like a zero (*sunya*) without any quantitative value. The quantitative aspect of the world-view having thus been eliminated, what now remains before his new eyes, born of *Sanyama*, is the interplay of the three energies (*gunas*) which constitutes the entire objective world, including all objects, animate and inanimate, not excluding the human organism. From now on it is this interplay of the three-fold energies that is seen to manifest itself in everything which happens to come within the range of his vision. He sees that every object in the active present is a product of the past; and it changes from moment to moment. Looking at the objects, or the objective world produces great activity (*vyuthana*) in the mind. He sees that the mind is a product of the past and that it is made up of impressions of bygone experiences. These impressions (*samskara*) are of two kinds: the impression of activity (out of which *vrttis* take shape), and impressions of non-activity or stillness (*nirodha*). And when the Yogi now looks at anything he finds that his mind oscillates between two poles: the pole of activity and the pole of non-activity or stillness. Seeing the oscillation he naturally inclines towards the pole of non-movement or *nirodha*. And as he does so repeatedly; the very force of this repeated action brings into being a quiet flow of the mind, which is the very negation of *vyuthana* or agitated activity (Sutra 10). This is the first transformation, called *nirodha-parinama*.

Sutra 11 describes the second transformation. The Yogi is now living with the quiet flow of the mind born of the first transformation (*nirodha-parinama*). As he so lives and looks at the world, he notices that another transformation takes place. The first transformation had negated the tendency of the mind always to hanker after this or that object, due to *vrtti-sarupya*. During the operation of this tendency the objective world, had got split up into fragments, each different from the other. With the ending of this tendency, the entire objective world, inclusive of all objects (*sarvartha*) converges on one point which operates as a focus through which the world, with all its differing objects, is seen as a whole, a totality, at a glance. It was this focus that came into being as a result of the first transformation (Sutras 9–10). And as the Yogi now looks at the world, he discovers that the mind is now oscillating between another kind of polarization: the pole of differing objects, at one end, and the pole of one-pointedness (*ekagrata*) inclusive of the totality of the objective world, at the other end. And, as he sees this oscillation, he finds that the totality of the objective world (*sarvarthata*) ends and vanishes from his view, and the all-inclusive one-pointedness (*ekagrata*) fills his whole field of vision. He inclines towards this one-pointedness. This constitutes the second transformation called *Samadhi-parinama*.

Sutra 11 describes the third transformation. As the Yogi repeatedly inclines toward the all-inclusive one-pointedness, he finds that the experience of quietude, on the one hand, and the experience of action arising from it, on the other, mutually equilibrate. They balance the inner quietude with the action started by a look at the world. It is as though the inner ecology of the psychosomatic organism were held in dynamic balance with the environmental ecology of the external world in every action of the Yogi. The stabilization in this perpetually dynamic ecological equilibrium brings into being the third and the last transformation, called *ekagrata-parinama*.

Sutra 13 says that these three transformations bring about corresponding transformations in the body (*bhuta*) and the senses (*indriya*) of the Yogi. The first transformation (Sutra 9) brings about a corresponding transformation in the very stuff or substance of which the body and the sense are made by nature. This is called *dharma-parinama*. The second transformation (Sutra 11) brings about a corresponding transformation in the temporal operations of the body and the senses of the Yogi. This is called *laksana-parinama*. The third transformation (Sutra 12) brings about a corresponding transformation in the very mechanism of which temporality is made. Temporality is nothing else but comprehension by an unsteady mind of the unending sequence of past–present–future in which the body and the senses get caught up. This appears to be an objective reality only so long as the mind remains caught up in *vrtti-sarupya*. But when the mind opts for *vrtti-nirodha* and undergoes the two transformations mentioned above, a third transformation takes place in the complex made up of the body and the senses, along with the third transformation in the mind mentioned in Sutra 12. This is called *avastha-parinama*, or transformation in the states of being of the body-senses complex on the one hand, and the objective world on the other. After this transformation, when the Yogi looks at the temporal world as a totality, its temporality undergoes a radical transformation and merges into a non-temporality of the Yogi's vision. This merging of temporality into the Yogi's non-temporal vision takes place after there has been disclosed to him the mystery of the entire mechanism of the temporal process – how it comes into being and how it ends up in timelessness.

It may be noted here that according to Yoga Darsana man's world-view is a product of the mind and of the body–senses complex in agitation or *vyutthana*, out of which *vrtti-sarupya* is born. When *vrtti-sarupya* end and *vrtti-nirodha* holds the scene, man opts for *astanga-yoga*. He then ceases to be a nature-made human being and becomes an authentic human being, or a Yogi. And it is this Yogi who witnesses the three transformations of the mind mentioned in Sutras 9, 11 and 12. He also sees that each of these three transformations brings about the three corresponding. transformations in his body–senses complex mentioned in Sutra 13. It is these transformations that radically alter the old world-view which was dominated by temporality, and brings into being a non-temporal world-view illumined by radiant wisdom (Sutra 5). The mind and the body–senses complex having undergone a radical transformation, a new and non-temporal world-view comes into being, because man's world-view depends on the states of his psychosomatic organism.

The Sutras that follow give an astounding description of what happens when the Yogi's new vision, charged with radiant wisdom, operates on the world through his action born of *Sanyama* (Sutra 4).

3
The World of Yogic Reality (1)

SUTRAS 14 TO 18

14. *Śāntoditāvyapadesyadharmānupātī dharmī*
A *dharmi* [one having characteristics] moves with and abides in three characteristics: stillness, arisenness and unnoticeableness.

15. *Kramānyatvaṁ pariṇāmānvatve hetuh*
The otherness of sequence is the cause of the otherness of effect or change.

16. *Parināmatrayasaṅyamādatītā-nāgatajñānaṁ*
Sanyama directed towards the three transformations results in the knowledge of that which has gone away and of that which is yet to arrive.

17. *Śabdārthapratyayānāmitaretarādhyāsātsaṅkarastatpra-vibhāga-saṅyamātsarvabhūtarutajñānaṁ*
False notions arising out of mistaking the word, the meaning [object] and the experience for each other, results in their intermixture and confusion; *Sanyama* directed towards each of these three as being distinct from one another, results in the knowledge of the sounds [language] of all beings.

18. *Saṅskārasākṣātkaraṇātpūrvajātijñānaṁ*
Direct perception of past impregnations [through *Sanyama*] results in the knowledge of past incarnations.

NOTES AND COMMENTS

As we have seen, Sutras 9 to 13 deal with three transformations of the mind and of the body-senses complex. The Sutras now before us (14 to 18) tell us what the Yogi sees by directing *Sanyama* (Sutra 4) towards various things, within and without. To direct *Sanyama* to things is to look at them with the eyes of the trinity of *dharana-dhayana-Samadhi* (Sutra 4)

Sutra 14 says that as a result of the three transformations mentioned in Sutras 9 to 13, the Yogi becomes aware of the fact that these transformations take place in the mind (*citta*) which is called *dharmi* in this Sutra (14). The Yogi sees that the mind is an entity which moves with and abides in its three characteristics, namely, stillness, inertness or being at rest (*santa*), arisenness or being in action (*udita*), and unnoticeableness (*avyapadesya*). Even a non-Yogi can be aware of these three characteristics (*dharmas*) of his mind. One can notice that the mind is either still and motionless; or it is active through ideation; or it is neither still nor active but remains a mystery about which nothing can be noticed or said. This latter is a characteristic which is, as it were, yet to come into being and assume a noticeable or observable form. This is called *anagata* or the unarrived (but capable of arriving) characteristic of the mind. It is also loosely described by non-Yogis as the 'future'. The arisen or active characteristic of the mind is known as the 'present'; and the stillness or inactivity of the mind is a characteristic which is commonly known as the 'past'.

All these three characteristics (*dharmas*) coexist in the mind; but they appear to be sequential and, therefore, temporal. We commonly assume that time or temporality is made up of the unending sequences of past, present and future. We remember something about our childhood, which we describe as the past. We see we are in the active present which endures from moment to moment. And we think that our body–senses complex (psychosomatic organism) will grow old, gradually lose its vitality and strength, and eventually end up in our death or non-being. This we call the future, or, in the words of the Sutras, *anagata* (that which is yet to arrive, but which is bound to arrive and overtake us). This body-based temporal consciousness is projected by man towards the outside world, which is therefore, assumed to be temporal by nature.

This understanding of time or temporality is so deeply ingrained in the human psyche that we are unable to see that what we call past, present and future are only innate characteristics of the mind about whose nature we actually know nothing. We project this body-based and mind-born temporality on to the world. We assume that everything is dominated by this temporality, and therefore, we believe that it is an objective reality, unchangeable, and existential imperative, the very condition of our being.

The Yogi sees through and beyond this mind-made temporality.

He does so because, firstly, he has opted for the discipline of Yoga; and secondly, because he has seen the above mentioned three transformations taking place in his mind and his body–senses complex. His vision and his world-view have therefore undergone a radical or mutational transformation. What he sees as a result of this transformation, both in his mind and in his body–senses complex, and through them in the world, is radically different from what we, as non-Yogis, see and comprehend. The point that Yoga Darsana drives home is that any man can see what a Yogi sees if he opts for the discipline of Yoga and lives with it totally. This point has to be constantly borne in mind in trying to understand what these and most other Sutras are trying to convey.

Sutra 14 speaks of mind as *dharmi* moving with and abiding in three characteristics: *santa, udita,* and *avyapadesya*. When the Yogi looks at the mind, as the *dharmi*, through the eyes of *Sanyama*, he becomes aware of these three characteristics in an instant. Then he directs his *Sanyama* on each of these three characteristics and discovers that the first one, *santa*, the inactive or inert state of the mind, is a product of past impregnations (*samskaras*), which in fact are *vyutthana samskaras* (mentioned in Sutra 9), and his Yogic glance at these past *samskaras* reveals to him the entire past that clings to the mind, through the operation of memory. The past is what has gone away, never to return. But it has left behind impressions which are imprinted on the mind-stuff. The mystery which these *samskaras* hide behind them is now revealed to the Yogi through *Sanyama*. Having thus gained the knowledge of the past, *atita*, he directs his *Sanyama* towards what is yet to arrive (or the future), i.e. *anagata*. This yogic look penetrates through the mind, which then reveals all that may come into being hereafter in respect of his psychosomatic organism. Sutra 16 speaks of this knowledge about the past and the future (*atita-anagata*).

How does the Yogi get this knowledge? Sutra 15 answers this question. It says that the psychosomatic organism, and everything that is seen and experienced through it, is a product of *krama*, or a certain sequence of events or moments (*ksana*). Everything in this world is a product or effect of such sequences. And, therefore, if one is able to see through this sequence in one's mind, one may totally transform it. The nature-made or the past-made sequence (*krama*) results in an inert characteristic (*santa*), which contains the past as a memory. But *Sanyama* directed towards this *santa* or inert mind, reveals its nature and structure as being the product of a certain sequence of events that have gone away. It reveals how this characteristic came to be what it is now. It reveals the interactions between the mind and the world that were experienced in the past and of which this *santa* came to be a product. In this manner it reveals past incarnations which one's mind underwent, as stated in Sutra 18. Thus the Yogi now understands the nature and structure of his psyche as it operates in the active present. And when he directs his *Sanyama* on what is yet to arrive, with which the mind will be later associated, he sees the sequence of moments and events which will lead up to this unarrived characteristic. In this way he becomes aware of the *anagata*. The Yogi becomes capable of acquiring knowledge of the past (*atita*) and the future (*anagata*) because of *Sanyama* directed towards the aforementioned three transformations. This is what Sutra 16 affirms. This affirmation is based on the fact that the 'seer', or pure seeing energy, when it ceases to see through past experiences, becomes free and capable of looking at them and beyond them, is thus able to discover the underlying sequences that resulted in giving the mind the characteristic of conditioned inertness. This inertness is here called *santa*.

It is pertinent to note that the three characteristics (*dharmas*) of the mind as the *dharmi*, mentioned in Sutra 14, are equivalent to the three characteristics of the 'seen' (*drsya*) or the objective world, mentioned in Part II-18. These are *sthiti, kriya* and *prakasa*. *Sthiti* or inertia is common to all material objects. In the case of the mind it assumes the form of an immaterial steady, called here *santa*. Similarly *kriya* assumes the form of arisenness (*udita*) and *prakasa* assumes the form of unnoticeableness or amorphousness (*avya-padesya*). In the view of Yoga Darsana, *citta* (the mind) is like an invisible bridge bringing the 'seer' and the 'seen' into contact. At the 'seer' end it is *citta* (the past passive participle of *cit* 'to see') and at the 'seen' end it is *drsya*, the observable object. The mind is thus a compound of two distinct cosmic energies: the energy of 'pure seeing', and the energy of the 'seen'. Hence the three characteristics of the 'seen' assume, in the case of the mind, the three different forms mentioned above.

The nature of the mind is later expounded in Part IV. There we are told that the mind (*citta*) as an existential entity (*dharmi*) is common to all beings, or species. In the case of the human species, the emergence of *asmita* ('I-am-ness') brings differences in each individual human being because of the different ways in which the choice-making propensity that is born of *asmita* (Part IV-2 to 5), operates in individuals. Sutra 23 of Part IV says that when the mind (*citta*) becomes passionately drawn towards the 'seer' and the 'seen', at one and the same time, it becomes capable of reflecting the entire objective world.

This being the existential situation with regard to the mind (*citta*), the three transformations mentioned in Sutras 9 to 12, and the corresponding transformations in the body–senses complex mentioned in Sutra 13, become possible through the discipline of Yoga. This is a discipline born of seeing and understanding the nature of the existential situation by man. Because of such transformations, it becomes possible for the Yogi to see, through his transformed mind, what is stated in Sutras 14 to 18, and much more besides as mentioned in later Sutras. These Sutras describe Reality as seen, felt and experienced by the Yogi. Yoga Darsana thus unfolds before our conditioned mind the immense hidden potentialities which the human mind harbours within its innermost core.

Sutra 17 speaks of word, meaning and experience, a trinity underlying the act of human experiencing, which forms the mechanism of communication, and which, in its turn, influences powerfully the nature and structure of common human consciousness. This common consciousness is confused, and therefore generates tensions and misery. The Yogi looks at this consciousness born of the complex trinity of word, meaning and experience. He looks at it with the eyes of *Sanyama* and discovers that the three factors of this trinity are three distinct entities, but that they tend to mix with each other and generate confusion and wrong notions about oneself and the objective world, through mistaking one for the other; and that, when they are seen as entities distinct from one another, a clear picture emerges in which the existential mechanism of communication, which is innate in all animate beings, as it were reveals its hidden mystery. With this revelation, all sounds of all beings (*sarvabhutaruta*) suddenly become intelligible to the Yogi, and thereafter, he finds himself in intelligent communion with existence as a whole.

The reference to sounds (*ruta*) in Sutra 17 has a very deep significance. The word as a sound is an articulated expression of the intention to communicate what has arisen in the mind. Similarly, the sounds of all animate beings represent their intention to communicate something that arises in their minds. This Sutra signifies that, existentially, the mechanism of communication and the process underlying the articulation of what arises in the mind-stuff is basically common to all beings, including man. Hence a clear understanding, through *Sanyama*, of the human mechanism of communication which is made up of the trinity of word–meaning–experience, naturally leads to the understanding of the communication mechanisms of all beings. The expression *sarva-bhuta-ruta* in the Sutra would include the sounds of even inanimate objects, because each of such objects when it produces sounds by friction with anything, has a sound distinct from all other sounds. It demands an extraordinary attention and exquisite sensitivity to distinguish these sounds from one another. It is this sensitivity of which the Sutra speaks.

Sutra 18 says that when the Yogi directly perceives (*saksatkaranat*) the complex mass of past impregnations (*samskaras*) on his mind-stuff, he distinctly sees the sequences (*krama*) which brought them into being. And tracing these sequences back to their origins, he reaches back to the previous incarnations through which his mind-stuff must have passed to carry the memory of experiences. The memories of these past incarnations are now mere static impregnations. The penetrating and inquiring look of the Yogi, charged with 'pure seeing' energy, as it were activates these impregnations (*samskaras*) so that they begin to unfold the sequences which brought them into being in the form of an imprinted record of past experiences.

In this connection it may be pertinent to refer to Sutra 33 of Part IV. This Sutra tells us what is meant by the word *krama*. *Krama* is that which is comprehended after looking at the effect produced by a succession of moments (*ksana*) which have now disappeared in the darkness of the past. When an effect becomes comprehensible, the succession of moments that produced it has already gone away. One can only see the effect but never the moments that produced it. This Sutra says that everything man sees is an effect of the past. And we become conscious of what is signified by the word 'past' only after looking at the effect which the succession of moments, has left behind. Time, in essence, is a mere succession of single moments (*ksana*), whose function is to produce observable effects, which are the objects we now see. We never see time as such. It is not perceivable at all. We infer its existence by looking at the effects it has produced in the form of objects, or imprints on the mind-stuff. And even this time whose existence we infer, is a matter of a sequence of single moments, a movement which always remains invisible. It is in fact the movement of the energy which manifests itself in the objective world. It is this world, full of solid objects of bewildering variety, that we see with our eyes.

The relation of a succession of moments to an effect is like the relation of energy to mass. Just as mass is convertible into energy so also an object or an effect is convertible into a succession, of moments by the Yogic energy of 'pure seeing'.

On the basis of this existential situation, it would be logical to say that if one can see through and beyond the object or the mass of impregnations on our mind-stuff, then the sequence of moments and events that have gone away after leaving their effects behind, could be perceived and traced back right to their origins. It is on the basis of this extraordinary perception that the Yogi becomes capable of knowing the past incarnations of his mind or egocentric self.

All this and much more that comes later in the following Sutras may appear fantastic and even incredible. But if one carefully follows the inner logic of the Yoga Sutras, the possibility of all these extraordinary perceptions of Reality (which, anyway always remains *the 'Great Unknown'* for all conditioned minds) is opened up before the eye of one's mind. After all, Reality is not a matter of knowing, but of being and seeing. And Yoga is a discipline that places man in a state of being in which alone direct perception of 'what is', of Reality, becomes possible. It is the world of Reality, perceivable only by the eyes of the Yogi, which is described in this Part.

4
The World of Yogic Reality (2)

SUTRAS 19 TO 22

19. *Pratyayasya (saṁyamāt) paracitta-jñānaṁ*
Sanyama directed towards an experience results in the knowledge of what is in the mind of others.

20. *Na ca Tatsālaṁbanaṁ tasyāviṣayībhūtatvāt*
The mind of the other cannot be the basis [of such knowledge] inasmuch as it cannot become the object of observation.

21. *Kāyarūpasaṁyamāttadgrāhya-śaktistaṁbhe cakṣuṣprakāśa-saṁyoge āṁtal rdhānaṁ*
By directing *Sanyama* on to the form of [his] body, the energy that makes it visible gets arrested, and the contact between the eyes and the rays of light [illuminating the body] is broken. This makes the body [of the Yogi] invisible [to others].

22. *Sopakramaṁnirupakramaṁ ca Karma tatsaṁyamādaparāṁta jñānamariṣṭebhyo vā*
Karma [activity] is of two kinds: one that has a beginning [and an end], and one that has no beginning [and no end]. *Sanyama* directed towards it [*karma*] results in the foreknowledge of [one's] death, through some misfortune.

NOTES AND COMMENTS

Sutra 19 says that the Yogi directing *Sanyama* on to an experience which he has of other men, through what they say, do or look like, acquires the knowledge of what is in their minds. Sutra 20 says that this knowledge is not based on a direct experiencing of the other's mind, but of its *vrttis* as expressed in words, deeds or gestures. The minds of other people cannot be directly experienced because they are invisible and therefore do not become objects of observation, experience or knowledge. But other people's minds have *vrttis* and when these are expressed in audible or visible forms they can be objects of experience. When this experience is subjected to *Sanyama* the Yogi can know what is in other men's minds. This is because every *vritti* has a *krama* (a particular sequence) behind it and, through *Sanyama*, the Yogi's power of perception can move back to the origin of the *vrtti* which has been expressed in a visible form.

Sutra 21 speaks of how the body of the Yogi can become invisible to others. The act of seeing an object involves a contact between the eyes and the rays of light illuminating the object. When the Yogi directs *Sanyama* towards the visible form of his body, the inner energy that makes the body radiate gets arrested. It is the combination of inner seeing energy and the external rays of light that makes one's body visible to others or to oneself. But when through *Sanyama*, the Yogi arrests the flow of his seeing energy going towards the form of his body, the body gets so darkened that it becomes incapable of reflecting the rays of external light. And, just as one cannot see anything in dense darkness, so also other people cannot see the body of the Yogi.

Sutra 22 tells us how a Yogi can foresee the time of his death through some accident. This becomes possible to the Yogi only when he directs *Sanyama* towards his *karma* or activity. *Karma*, says the Sutra, is of two kinds: (i) one that has a beginning and therefore an end, and (ii) one that has no beginning and therefore no end. *Sanyama* is action that has no cause, no beginning, and no end. Therefore, *Sanyama* directed towards his *karma* reveals to the Yogi the sequence (*krama*) of moments which results in an effect. This effect may be the death of the Yogi's body through some misfortune that may overtake him. Here the logic is the same as that of Sutra 15.

SUTRAS 23 TO 55

23. *Maitryādiṣu (saṅyamāt) balāni*

Sanyama directed towards friendliness [and the other three feelings mentioned in I–33] results in four kinds of strength or power [*maitri*, *karuna*, *mudita* and *upeksa*].

24. *Baleṣu hastibalādīni*

Sanyama directed towards strength itself results in physical powers, like the power of an elephant.

25. *Pravṛttyālokanvāsatsūkṣmavyavahitaviprakṛṣṭajñānaṁ*

Sanyama directed towards the illumination inherent in an intense *vrtti* results in knowledge of subtle [invisible] things, of things hidden or covered up, and of things far away.

26. *Bhuvanajñānaṁ Sūrye Saṅyamāt*

Sanyama directed towards the sun results in knowledge of the worlds [or the cosmos].

27. *Candre (saṅyamāt) tārāvyūhajñānaṁ*

Sanyama directed towards the moon results in knowledge of the complex arrangement of the stars.

28. *Dhruve (saṅyamāt) tadgatijñānaṁ*

Sanyama directed towards the Pole Star, known as Dhruva, results in knowledge of the velocities or movements of stars.

29. *Nābhicakre (saṅyamāt) kāyāvyūhajñānaṁ*

Sanyama directed towards the solar plexus [of one's body] results in the knowledge of the inner structural arrangement of one's body.

30. *Kaṅṭhakūpe (saṅyamāt) kṣutpipāsānivṛttin*

Sanyama directed towards the hollow of one's throat results in the disappearance of thirst and hunger.

31. *Kūrmanadyām (saṅyamāt) sthairyaṁ*

Sanyama directed towards the tortoise-shaped hollow in the lower region of the throat results in stability and firmness of mind.

32. *Mūrdhajyotiṣi (saṅyamāt) siddhadarśanaṁ*

Sanyama directed towards the luminous portion under the crown of the head results in the vision of the *siddhas* [invisible Masters or Perfect Yogis].

33. *Prātibhātvā sarvaṁ*

Or, everything becomes intelligible through the spark of genius [self-luminous knowledge].

34. *Hṛdaye (saṅyamāt) cittasaṁvit*

Sanyama directed towards the interior of the heart results in the understanding of one's mind.

35. *Satvapuruṣayoratyaṅtāsaṅ-kīrṇayoh pratyayāviśeṣo bhogah parārthātsvārtha saṅyamāt puruṣajñānaṁ*

The essence of one's psychosomatic being [*satva*] and the manness [*purusa*] within, are totally distinct from one another. Non-distinct and confused experience of the two is called *bhoga* because it is experiencing that which exists for the benefit of others. *Sanyama* directed towards that which exists for its own self results in the knowledge of *purusa* [the inner manness of man].

36. *Tatah prātibhaṣrāvaṇavedanā-darśāswādavārtā jāyañte*

As a result [of the knowledge of *purusa*], self-luminous extra-sensory perception comes into being, whereby one hears, feels, sees, tastes and smells that which is beyond the range of the ordinary senses.

37. *Te samādhāvupasargā vyutthāne siddhayah*

These [*siddhis*] are harmful to and subversive of *Samadhi* and appear like supernatural powers only when one is in a state of great mental activity [*vyutthana*], on the phenomenal level.

38. *Baṅdhakāraṇaśaithilyātpracāra-saṁvedanācca cittasya para-śarīrāveśah*

When [through *Sanyama*] the cause of bondage is loosened and the movement of sensitivity is set in motion, the mind becomes capable of entering into other bodies.

39. *Udānajayājjala paṅkakaṅtakādiṣvasaṅga utkrāṅtiśca*

Mastery over the upgoing [*udan*] breath enables the Yogi to walk through water, mud, thorns, etc. without being affected by them; it also enables the Yogi to ascend upward [levitation].

40. *Samānajayajjvalanaṁ*

Mastery over the *samana* breath results in making the body incandescent.

41. *Śrotrākāśayoh saṁbandha-saṅyamāddivyaṁ śrotraṁ*

Sanyama directed towards the relationship between the ear and the vast empty space [*akasa*] around it results in the acquisition of a divine sense of hearing.

42. *Kāyākāśayoh saṁbaṅdha-saṅyamāllaghutūlasamāpatteścā-kāśagamanaṁ*

Sanyama directed towards the relationship between the body and the empty space [*akasa*] around it, results in the body being reduced to the weightlessness of floating fibre or particles, and thereby enables the Yogi to travel freely in space.

43. *Bahirakalpitā vṛttirmahāvidehā tatah prakāśāvaraṇakṣayah*

The non-ideational state of mind moving outside is called the great bodiless *vrtti*; this *vrtti* removes the coverings over the self-luminous intelligence.

44. *Sthūl svarūpasūkṣmānvayārthavatvasaṅyamādbhūtajayah*

Sanyama directed towards the grossness, self-existence, subtleness, relatedness, and meaningfulness [of things] results in mastery over the material world.

45. *Tato-ṇimādiprādurbhāvah kāyasaṁpattaddharmānabhighā-taśca*
Thereby come into being *siddhis* [Yogic accomplishment] such as reducing one's body to the size of an atom [*anima*] and others, the excellence of the body, and power to remain unharmed by the qualities of material forces.

46. *Rūpalāvaṇya balavajrasaṅhananatvāni kāyasaṁpat*
The excellence of body [*kayasampat*] means being endowed with beauty, charm, strength and indestructibility [like *vajra*].

47. *Grahaṇasvarūpāsmitānvayārthavatva saṅyamādttiṅdriyajayah*
Sanyama directed towards the following five; namely, that through which things are received inside [*grahana*]; that which constitutes one's uniqueness [*svarupa*]; the feeling of 'I-am-ness' [*asmita*]; relatedness; and meaningfulness, results in mastery over the senses.

48. *Tato manojavitvaṁ vikaraṇabhāvah pradhānajayaśca*
Mastery over the senses results in a mindlike swiftness of bodily movements; in the ability to move freely from the origins to the termination of things irrespective of time, space and circumstances; and in mastery over the main essence of being [*pradhana*].

49. *Satvapuruṣānyatākhyātimātrasva sarvabhāvādhiṣṭhātṛtvaṁ sarvajñātṛtvaṁ ca*
One established in the pure vision of the total distinction between the essence of one's being [*satva*] and the manness within [*purusa*], becomes the basic ground of all things and of all-knowingness.

50. *Tadvairāgyādapi doṣabījakṣaye kaivalyaṁ*
Through disinterestedness [*vairagya*] even in that consummation, and with the total destruction of the seeds of impurity, there comes into being total freedom.

51. *Sthānyupanimaṅtraṇe saṅgasmayākaraṇam punaraniṣṭa prasaṅgāt*
When entertained by those established in social conformity, the Yogi gets neither contaminated by it nor astonished by it even though he may be treated with great deference and high honour; because to do so would repeatedly result in undesirable consequences.

52. *Kṣaṇatatkramayoh saṅyamādvivekajaṁ jñānaṁ*
Sanyama directed towards moments and their sequences results in the knowledge which is born of discerning [existential] intelligence.

53. *Jātilakṣaṇadeśairanyatā-navacchedāttulyayostatah pratipattih*

Perception born of such knowledge penetrates through things indistinguishable from each other because of the commonness of species, location, time, and soil and is able to distinguish them from each other.

54. *Tārakam sarvaviṣayaṁ sarvathāviṣayamakramaṁ ceti viveka-jaṁ jñānaṁ*

Knowledge born of *viveka* [discerning existential intelligence] is creative [*tarakam*], is capable of comprehending everything, in every manner, and is without sequences of time [i.e. instantaneous].

55. *Satva-puruṣayeh śuddhisāmye kaivalyamiti*

When total purity in *satva* or the essence of being equals the total purity in *purusa* or manness within, then total freedom comes into being.

NOTES AND COMMENTS

A precise understanding of all the Sutras in Part III that speak of the emergence of extraordinary powers, or seemingly supernatural phenomena must be left to the meditational insight of the readers who care to opt for the discipline of Yoga. But it seems necessary to draw attention to some basic points in this connection in order to facilitate right understanding.

First and foremost, none of these *siddhis* or extraordinary powers are the results of any egocentric effort or practice on the part of a Yogi or anybody else. The reason for this is that these are *siddhis* born of *Samadhi* and *Sanyama*. And *Samadhi* is not an achievement, accomplishment or attainment acquired through effort. Even *viveka-khyati* (II-26, 27) helps one only up to the first seven stages or *angas* of the eight-fold way of Yoga. Sutra 45 of Part II specifically lays down that the *siddhi* of *Samadhi* comes into being only through the grace of God. This grace may come only if one understands and become one with God-awareness, as described in I-23 to 29.

Secondly, all these *siddhis* come into being when *Sanyama* is directed towards certain things. This direction takes place spontaneously and not through any egocentric efforts. This is clear from Sutra 6 of Part III. The Yogi does not do this; it happens. Therefore, all these *siddhis* are happenings, and not creations of effort.

Thirdly, *Sanyama* is a trinity, that is, three things operating together. These three are *dharana, dhyana* and *samadhi* (III-1 to 3). Therefore a Yogi, who has to live in this world, must necessarily see, hear and feel things that happen all around him. But he may or may not attend to them. If he does attend to them, this naturally results in the energy of his attention being directed towards certain things. But before this happens, the Yogi's mind must already have undergone three transformations, accompanied by the corresponding three transformations in his body and senses (Sutra 9 to 13). Therefore, when his attention is drawn by anything around him it is an attention charged with the energy of this body-mind complex combined with the three-fold transformation. He looks at things which draw his attention to them. First he looks with the eyes of *dharana* or total emptiness of mind bound by a void-like space; secondly, he looks with the eyes of a single experience of emptiness with which he is totally in harmony (*dhayana*); and thirdly, he looks with the eyes of the suddenly emerging *Samadhi*, in which his identity is stripped of all attributes (*svarupa-sunyata*), and the radiant objective reality, unfolds itself and occupies the whole field.

It is now the radiance of this all-pervading Reality, working through his eyes, and penetrating what he looks at which holds the attention of the Yogi. This is *Sanyama*. It is this Radiant Reality, operating not only through the eyes but also through the whole being of the Yogi, that reveals the basic truth underlying all things, namely, that everything in this world, *except the energy of 'pure seeing'* is a product of a certain sequence of moments and events that have disappeared in the darkness of the past. The eyes of the Yogi, charged with the energy of *Sanyama*, which is the only thing ever remaining unaffected by temporality, activates the sequence of moments and events that lie beneath and within every visible object. In this manner, the past (*atita*) and the future (*anagata*) sequences are revealed to him (Sutras 15 and 16).

This is what happens with regard to everything mentioned in these Sutras. Therefore, all these extraordinary, and seemingly supernatural events, are mere happenings which are natural to the transcendental vision of the Yogi.

Lastly, the point always to be borne in mind is that the whole movement of Yoga Darsana (the world-view of Yoga) converges on a single consummation. This is *kaivalya* or total freedom. It begins to take shape (if it has any shape) with one basic perception, described in Sutra 35. This Sutra tells us that every experience of man is a *bhoga*, or self-indulgence. It is so because he remains unaware of the fact that the 'seer' in his being, the very manness of man (*purusa*), is totally distinct from his psychosomatic organism which constitutes his being. This 'being' is the 'seen' and not the 'seer'. The two can never be one and the same thing, although they are close to each other. They live together. But although they are physically inseparable, existentially they are always distinct from each other. The perception of this truth, which is instantaneous and devoid of temporal sequence, is basic to freedom (*kaivalya*). It is basic to a radiant clarity of vision. That vision which is born from confusing the 'seer' and the 'seen' as if they were one and the same thing is the clouded vision (*avidya-khyati*) of all men who have not wholeheartedly opted for the discipline of Yoga. This confusion results in *bhoga* or self-indulgence. On the other hand the vision born of a clear distinction between the two, leads to the right understanding of the manness of man (*purusa-jnanam*, Sutra 35). This brings about the loosening of bondage (Sutra 38), and is the first and last decisive step towards freedom.

With this loosening of all bondages born of the past, two things begin to happen: (i) purity of being (*satva*); and (ii) purity of the manness in the being of man (*purusa*). The being of man becomes the ground for the free and full reception of all things and all experiences or knowledge. This happens because man has now become *satva-purusanyata-khyatimatra*–a matter of pure awareness of the distinction between the 'seer' and the 'seen', between the manness in man, on the one hand, and his being in the form of his psychosomatic organism on the other. Since everything in this immense universe exists, so far as man is concerned, only in an through what is received within by way of the senses and the mind, man becomes the ground for the reception of all things, and therefore of all-knowingness (Sutra 49). But this all-knowingness must not degenerate into any form of egoism. When one sees this danger one loses interest even in this wondrous all-knowingness. It may or may not be there. After one has once seen the radiant truth of all things nothing else matters. Thus *vairagya* or disinterestedness even in all-knowingness, burns away all the seeds of impurity, both in the being of man and in the manness within it. Total and equal purity of both is total freedom (Sutra 55). This is the consummation of man as a product of nature into an existentially authentic human being. This is MAN whose being and living always abides in total freedom. This is man transformed into a Yogi.

One thing more. Sutra 37 lays down that *siddhis* are harmful to *Samadhi*. If one who is on the path of Yoga, gets caught up in the wondrous thrills of *siddhis*, he loses touch with *Samadhi*, and is then thrown back into the corrupting quagmire of the non-Yogic way of living. A real, authentic Yogi will never be an exhibitionist, demonstrating his extraordinary powers. Those who do so and get the applause of the crowds all over the world who delight in sensations are not Yogis, whatever else they may be. In fact they are the destroyers and perverters of the discipline of Yoga. For century upon century Yoga has come to be equated with the demonstrable acquisition of *siddhis*. This is a lie and a blasphemy against Yoga.

PART FOUR

Kaivalya Pada

1
Nature and Man

SUTRAS 1 TO 13

1. *Janmouṣadhi-mantra-tapah-samadhijāh siddhayah*
Extraordinary accomplishments [*siddhis*] are either inborn, or born of medicinal herbs or of incantation, or of austerity, or of *Samadhi*.

2. *Jātyàntarapariṇamah prakṛtyāpūrāt*
Mutational transformations of species take place as a result of the overflow of nature.

3. *Nimittamaprayojakaṁ prakṛtīnāṁ varaṇabhedastu tatah kṣetrikavat*
[Man-made] instrumental or efficient cause can neither originate nor maintain the natural entities. Man differs [from all other natural entities] by reason of choice-making. He is like a farmer who turns the flow of the natural river-water to his fields [by letting in a canal].

4. *Nirmāṇacittāni asmitāmātrat*
Individualized minds are wholly the [ideational] creations of 'I-am-ness' [*asmita*].

5. *Pravṛttibhede prayojakaṁ cittamekamanekeṣāṁ*
The [nature-made] mind that motivates differences in individualized minds is common to all men.

6. *Tatra dhyānajamanāśayaṁ*
There [among differing individual minds] that mind which is born of meditation is devoid of the residue of past impressions.

7. *Karmāśuklākṛṣṇaṁ Yoginastrividhamitareṣām*
The actions of the Yogi are neither bright [virtuous] nor dark [vicious], but the actions of men other than Yogis are of three kinds [bright, dark and mixed].

8. *Tatastadvipākānuguṇānāmevā-bhivyaktirvāsanānāṁ*

The built-in impressions [*vasana*] of the three kinds of actions [left on the minds of non-Yogis] manifest themselves wholly in accordance with their characteristics or qualities, and ripen into effects which are inherent in them.

9. *Jātideśakālavyavahitānāmapyānantaryaṁ smṛtisaṅskārayorekarūpatvāt*

The built-in impressions, even though separated or placed apart by conditions of birth, space and time, remain close together because memory [*smrti*, which is here and now] and the built-in impressions [*sanskaras*, which are there and then] are of the same kind.

10. *Tāsāmanāditvaṅ cāa-śiṣonityatvāt*

And they are beginningless because wishfulness, which is inherent in them, is perpetual and endless.

11. *Hetuphalāṣrayālambanaih sangṛhītatvadeṣāmabhave tadabhāvah*

Motivation, fruits resulting from it, the supporting material and dependence – the acceptance of these four factors maintains the continuity of memory-impressions. The negation of these four factors results in the negation of *karma* [actions].

12. *Atītānāgataṁ svarūpato-styadhvabhedāddharmāṇām*

That which has gone away [*atita*] and that which is yet to arrive [*anagata*], both remain in existence along with their identities. This fact can be inferred from the differences in their temporal characteristics [which leave their marks on the material in which their operations take place].

13. *Te vyaktasūkṣma guṇātmānah*

They [the characteristics] are either manifest or unmanifest [subtle].

NOTES AND COMMENTS

This is the fourth and last Part of Yoga Darsana. It is entitled *Kaivalya Pada*. The word *kaivalya* is traditionally taken to mean 'freedom'. But this Yogic freedom is quite distinct from all other notions of freedom. In fact, it is not a mental construct, or a mental build-up, a notion, an idea, a concept, an ideal, or an end to be pursued. Nor is it freedom *from* anything. It is the existential core of man's manness, to be discovered and realized by his negating everything that prevents pure perception of 'what is'.

This is what the word *kaivalya* itself indicates. The word is derived from *kevala* which means 'one and only, alone'. *Kaivalya* thus means 'aloneness'. This is an existential description of the very condition of man's manness. Man is intrinsically alone in the midst of the alien and bewildering multitude of objects all around him.

Man regards himself as the 'I' who is not and can never be, 'not-I' or the 'other'. And yet this man, with his innate sense of 'I-am-ness' (*asmita*), which in fact is aloneness, must live together with everything that constitutes the other, or otherness. This also is a condition of man's existence. He must breathe, eat, and drink for his very survival. He must see, hear, touch, taste and smell that which is not, and can never be the 'I'. He must tend to experience pleasure or pain in respect of everything that the senses offer for his benefit. And he must experience at all times the presence of the mysterious immensity of the world around him, so utterly alien and yet so vital for his existence. This existential necessity of experiencing the other, or otherness, forms the very essence of togetherness, or relatedness. 'To be is to be related.'

This is the existential situation in which man finds himself. It is a three-fold complex of 'I-am-ness', otherness and togetherness. Or, to put it differently, it is a trinity of aloneness, alienness, and relatedness. If this be so, how can aloneness or *kaivalya* imply freedom? Ordinarily, or viewed uncritically, it seems to imply nothing but dependence. And this is exactly what man assumes, right from his birth. To begin with, he starts with dependence on parents, then on society and its so-called leaders, and then on nature and the objective world. But this assumption of dependence and the way of living dominated by it, inevitably leads man into tensions, conflicts, sorrow, misery and chaos. And it is only when man gets confronted with this existential despair that he is totally thrown back on himself and is compelled to face the fact of his utter aloneness. This is perception of the first aspect of the three-fold existential situation. It demands right understanding of 'I-am-ness' or aloneness, alienness or otherness, and togetherness or relatedness. This understanding leads to the discipline of Yoga, as expounded in the last three Parts. This exposition of the existential situation enables one to understand the real significance of 'I-am-ness', otherness and togetherness in existential terms. First and foremost, it breaks asunder the ideational oneness of 'I-am-ness' (II-6). It brings one to face the fact that the body-bound sense of 'I-am-ness' is a nature-made entity, like any other object. Bereft of the support of one's body–mind complex, the sense of 'I-am-ness' gets shorn of all substance and attributes, and is reduced to the status of a mere word-generated knowledge, which is *vrtti* or ideation and as such devoid of reality (I-9). Stripped naked of the covering of the body–mind complex and its ideational or mental operations (*vrttis*), one is left with 'pure seeing', from moment to moment. In this state there is no egocentric entity to accumulate and get entangled in experiences and their impressions on the mind-stuff or the brain cells.

This extraordinary 'pure seeing' is named the 'seer' – the central core of man's manness in the existential sense (II-20). This is aloneness with total freedom in the sense of total disentanglement from being confused ideationally with the flow of nature (*prakrtyapura*) and the entire objective world, which constitutes the 'seen' for the 'seer'. This is aloneness free from the egocentric 'I-am-ness' along with its tensions-breeding activities. It is now aloneness charged with the 'energy of pure seeing', and is thus capable of free inquiry into the nature and structure of the existential situation. It is now aloneness as an integral aspect of and co-extensive with existence as a whole. It is now aloneness in a state of creative harmony with the objective world – creative because of freedom from the past, or temporality. The mystery underlying universal relatedness or togetherness now begins to unfold itself before one's eyes – eyes which are now charged with the inherently free energy of pure seeing. This is *kaivalya* or the freedom of the 'seer' (II-25).

It is pertinent to note here that the Yoga Darsana uses only the word *kaivalya* to signify freedom, and no other synonym, such as *svatantrya, svadhinata, mukti* or *moksa*. All these synonyms miss the existential foundation of freedom, and hence tend to make freedom a matter of ideation, an end to be pursued, or a goal to be attained through the process of time. The word *kaivalya*, on the other hand, implies freedom founded on the existential fact of man's aloneness in the midst of the bewildering multitude of objects around him. To understand, not through duration but through instantaneous perception, the existential and non-temporal significance of aloneness otherness and togetherness is to realize and live in freedom from moment to moment.

Similarly, it is pertinent to note that the Yoga Darsana uses only the word *purusa* to signify man, and no other synonym such as *manava* or *manusya*. These latter miss the existential essence of man's manness. They emphasize the mental or ideational aspects of man which are confused with *vrttis*, to the detriment of the existential core of man's manness. The word *purusa*, on the other hand, brings out precisely the existential significance of man's manness. This word *purusa* is derived from *puri-saya* which means 'reposing in a city, a town, or a body'. The manness of man signifies that which reposes in his body, but is quite distinct from it. Although this reposing manness, slumbering or awake, is physically *inseparable* from the body or the psychosomatic organism of man, it is clearly *distinguishable* from it. To perceive this existential distinction is to be truly intelligent and authentically human. On the other hand, not to perceive this existential distinction, and not to live a life grounded in this perception, is to cease to be an authentic human being and to live a life dominated and endlessly distorted by the blind and unintelligent forces of the past which constitute one's natural and social heritage. This is exactly what has been expounded in the last three Parts.

In this fourth and the last Part we are brought face to face with three things: the flow of nature, the stuff of which the mind is made, and the absolute necessity of a total transformation of one's mind. The logic underlying Sutras 1 to 13 runs as follows:

1. Men are born with some powers of varying degrees. In fact all objects in this world, animate and inanimate, are pregnant with powers or potential energy. Without inquiring into and trying to understand the *raison d'être* of these inborn powers men tend to use them to get the better of their neighbours and other fellow beings. With this object they are always seeking extraordinary powers. These are called *siddhis*. Sutra 1 says that *siddhis* are either inborn, or when they are not inborn, that they are acquired through medicinal herbs, or through words charged with magical powers, or through austerity associated with this or that discipline, or through Yogic meditation and *Samadhi*. These five sources of *siddhis* seem to be merely illustrative and not exhaustive. There could be other ways through which extraordinary powers or capacities could be acquired as, for instance through science and technology – the craze of modern times. The point that is driven home in the following Sutras is this: no amount of such *siddhis* or extraordinary powers, acquired by means, whatever can solve the problem of the survival or the enrichment of the human in man. The only way to approach the problems that perpetually confront man is the way of understanding the existential significance of three things, namely, aloneness, otherness and togetherness and then living and acting in the light of such understanding.

2. Sutra 2 states that the mutational transformations of species are brought about by the 'flow of nature' (*prakrtyapura*). Man himself belongs to one of such species. It is not given to him to bring about a radical transformation in his nature-made biological organism. All that is given to him is to see, understand and make peace with this existential situation. But he cannot do this unless and until he brings about a radical transformation in his own being on the basis of what is given to him.

3. Sutra 3 says that no man-made or any other cause (*nimitta*) can either originate or maintain the 'flow of nature'. All that man can do is to utilize the 'flow of nature' to his advantage, as the farmer utilizes the flow of the nature-made river to irrigate his fields by digging a canal. This is all that is given to man. But its potentialities are tremendous if man cares to respect and understand the existential situation. Man differs from all that is nature-made in one respect: his ability to choose (*varana-bheda*). Therefore, the existential situation demands that man must explore the immense potentialities of this unique ability. He must not fritter away in petty trivialities the tremendous energy potential that this ability to choose hides within its core. This potential is co-equal and coextensive with the threefold cosmic energies that originate and maintain the flow of nature and the ecological order of the universe.

4. Man must never lose sight of the fact that all individualized minds are the ideational creations of the built-in sense of 'I-am-ness' as stated in Sutra 4. The unique ability to choose operates through this sense of 'I-am-ness' (*asmita*). And man will never realize and actualize the mighty energy potential that inheres in his being unless he sees the fact that this sense of 'I-am-ness' is not unitary but a fusion of two distinct cosmic energies (II-6). Unless the egocentric workings of this fusion are carefully observed with choiceless awareness, and the distinction between the energy that is the 'seer' and the energy that is the 'seen' is clearly understood and assimilated, there is no hope for man. In the absence of this understanding he can only invite more and more trouble and eventual disaster.

Man must also see the fact that although individual choices differ from each other, the mind-stuff out of which these varying choices emerge is common to all men. It is this nature made mind-stuff that motivates individualized minds, through built-in likes and dislikes and other tendencies. This is what Sutra 5 makes clear. Inattention to this fact can only perpetuate division between man and man, and man and nature and end up in inevitable conflict and its relentless result of confusion, chaos and destruction.

5. One who sees all these facts and respects them, will hold himself back and cease to choose and be a victim of his choices. This brings about a radical break in the past-propelled continuity and results naturally in the discipline of Yoga. It brings about a mutational transformation of the mind. It is not given to man to bring about mutational transformations in the biological species. But it is open to man to bring about a mutational transformation in his own mind. This, according to Yoga, is the *raison d'être* of man's existence. This whole misery to which man has become heir is the result of his neglect of this existential situation.

An individual mind that has undergone such a radical transformation is called *dhyanaja-citta* in Sutra 6. It is described as *anasaya*. The word *asaya* means 'a resting place', 'an asylum', 'a receptacle, reservoir'. The nature-made mind is a reservoir of past impressions of varying and conflicting experiences. It is therefore full of inner tensions (*klesa*). All actions motivated by this past-ridden mind which is common to all men, take three forms: bright or virtuous; dark or vicious; and a mixture of the two; whereas the actions that emerge from the mind of Yogi are neither bright nor dark. They have a different dimension altogether (Sutra 7). The mind of Yogi is called *dhyanaja-citta* or a mind born of meditation and become *anasaya*. *Anasaya* means devoid of all vestiges of the accumulated impressions of the past. Consequently, the actions of a Yogi radically differ from the activities of non-Yogi, or the common men whose minds are overwhelmingly dominated by *asaya*, the refuge of the past which motivates their actions. These actions of non-Yogis take three forms, as has already been stated (Sutra 7). These three kinds of actions sow their respective seeds in the mind-stuff and these ripen in accordance with the characteristics or qualities (*gunas*) germane to them. These seeds are called *vasanas*. The word *vasana* means 'knowledge derived from memory, particularly, the impressions unconsciously left on the mind by good or bad actions done in the past'. The past lingers in the present through memory. Memory is made up of the impressions of past experiences and actions. Consequently, although these built-in past impressions may be separated by time, place and conditions of birth they remain close together in the mind-stuff. This is so because of the identity of memory (*smrti*) and past impressions (*samskara*). This is what is stated in Sutra 9.

Sutra 10 says that these *vasanas* (past impressions) are beginningless because of the endless desire (*asis*), inherent in them.

What then is one to do? Sutra 11 answers this question. It says that if one cares to find out how the past-propelled wheel of *karma* is kept perpetually going by *asis*, one will discover that this movement involves four factors, namely egocentric motive (*hetu*); the fruits resulting from it; the material that supports these fruits, and dependence on this material. One who discovers these four factors which underlie the movement of *karma* also finds a way whereby the wheel will slow down and eventually come to a stop. This way is the way of negation (*abhava*). Cease to choose and to motivate the wheel of *karma*. This negative action will prevent the germination of the seeds of actions. When there is no germination, the material supporting germination will remain sterile. This will negate the tendency to depend on any material or external object.

This process of negating the four factors underlying the actions of non-Yogis leads to a momentous discovery. It is discovery that unveils the mystery underlying time as the past and the future. The past (*atita*) continues to exist in the present through the memory of impressions of past experiences and actions, which forms the unconscious stuff of the mind. And the future, which is yet to arrive (*anagata*), is already in this unconscious stuff of the mind, as the fruit is in the seed. A mango seed must necessarily produce a mango fruit, and no other. And although the seed is the product of the past, it carries within its stuff the fruit which will arrive in future. This future, being determined by the past, exists in the present in the material stuff of the seed. The way of the past and the way of the future differ only in their directions (*adhva-bheda*). But the material on the basis of which the past and the future operate in their respective ways retains its identify (*svarupa*) at all times. Movement, which is the distinguishing feature of time or temporality, necessarily implies movement of an object or a substance. If there be no object there could be no movement and therefore no time as either past or the future.

Therefore energy (of which objects are forms), becoming aware of itself in man, sees through differing movements of the past or the future and thus gets liberated from identification with them. Such liberated awareness is non-temporal.

Sutra 13 says that the characteristics of an object, or the objective world, are either manifest (*vyakta*) or unmanifest, i.e. subtle and invisible (*suksma*). That which is in its own identity (*svarupatah asti*,

Sutra 12) is either manifest and visible, or subtle and invisible. This is so because it is composed of *gunas* or the complex of the three-fold energies mentioned in II-18. It is a complex of these three-fold energies (*gunas*) constantly interacting with one another that makes objects manifest or clear to the eye or mind. When there is no such manifestation the material stuff (the three-fold energies) of which objects are made remains unmanifest or invisible. The material stuff although unmanifest or invisible, still continues to exist. It never ceases to exist.

This brings us face to face with 'what is', or the stuff out of which the universe is made. The following Sutras, discussed in the next chapter, throw light on this 'stuff', which is entitled *vastu* or reality.

2
Man, Mind and the World

SUTRAS 14 TO 24

14. *Pariṇāmaikatvāt-vastutatvam*
The principle underlying the objectivity of an object or the objective world [*vastu*] lies in one thing only, that is, perpetual change.

15. *Vastusāmye cittabhedāttayor vibhaktah panthāh*
Whereas *vastu* remains the same the ways of the *vastu* and of the individualized minds [*citta*] are different and move away from each other.

16. *Na caikacittatantram vastu tadapramāṇakaṁ tadā kiṁ śyāt*
The *vastu* is not subservient to an individual mind because this has no validity; if this be so, what then [what is one to do]?

17. *Taduparāgāpeksitvāccittasya vastu jñātājñātaṁ*
The *vastu* becomes known or remains unknown, depending on the mind's passion for it.

18. *Sadā jñātāṣcittavṛttayastatprabhoh puruṣasyāpariṇāmitvāt*
The *citta-vrttis* are always known to their lord [man or *purusa*] because *purusa* does not undergo any change [as *vrttis* do].

19. *Na tatsvābhāsaṁ dṛśyatvāt*
Citta is not self-luminous because it is observable [the 'seen'].

20. *Ekasamaye cobhayānava-dhāraṇaṁ*
The mind cannot ascertain or determine both [*vastu* and *purusa*] at one and the same time.

21. *Cittāntaradṛśye buddhibuddherati-prasaṅgah smṛtisaṅkaraṣca*
If one were to assume that one mind is observable by another mind, and this another by yet another, and so on, intelligence would reach a state of *reductio ad absurdum*, and also cause confusion and chaos of memories.

22. *Citerapratisaṅkramāyāstadā-kārapattau svabuddhisaṁ-vedanaṁ*

The 'seer' [*cit*] while face to face with the form of an object received by the mind, does not get altered in any way by it but becomes aware of its intelligence [through the quiet mind-stuff reflecting the object].

23. *Draṣṭṛdṛśyoparaktaṁ cittaṁ sarvārthaṁ*

When the mind [in a steady state] reflects both the 'seer' and the 'seen', in the colours of each other's identity, it becomes inclusive of all objects [through their knowledge].

24. *Tadasaṅkhyeyavāsanābhiṣcitramapi parārthaṁ saṅhatyakāritvāt*

Although the mind gets coloured by innumerable impressions [*vāsanā*] it still remains an object for the benefit of some one other than itself [*purusa*], because it gathers mass due to its identification with many objects.

NOTES AND COMMENTS

A non-Yogi (an ordinary man) whose actions take three forms – bright, dark and a mixture of both – and who discovers that all his actions are egocentrically motivated, comes to realize sooner or later what has been described in Sutras 7 to 13, and discussed in the previous chapter. One who comes upon this realization suddenly becomes aware of the fact that the principle underlying the objectivity of an object, or the objective world (*vastu*), lies in one thing, and one only. It is perpetual change (*parinama*). *Vastu* would ever remain incomprehensible and unknown if its existence did not take a form clearly perceptible by the eye or the mind. That is to say *vastu* has to appear in a perceptible form in order to declare its existence to an observer. This can happen only if *vastu* undergoes a change from moment to moment and becomes solid enough to be seen. This is the manifestation of *vastu*. *Vastu* is either manifest or unmanifest. Everything we see and become aware of is seen to undergo perpetual change. A fresh flower, seen after a lapse of time, appears to have lost its freshness. It has undergone a change by sheer passage of time. A shining piece of cloth kept in a box and then taken out after a year or so, is seen to have lost its radiance by sheer passage of time. Time is that which goes on from moment to moment, producing effects or changes. And the accumulated effect of many moments becomes an object perceptible to the eye or the mind. This is the manifestation of that which we call by the name 'object'. Again, everything so manifested undergoes a change from moment to moment, until at last that which was manifest becomes unmanifest again.

Objectivity thus consists of movement in time, from the unmanifest to the manifest, and then from the manifest to the unmanifest. This constitutes the existential nature of all objects and of the objective world as a whole. This is what Sutra 14 means and implies.

What then is mind? Is it an object (*vastu*)? Or is it something other than an object?

This question is answered in Sutras 15 to 17.

We are already told in Sutras 4 and 5 that all individualized minds are the creations of *asmita* ('I-am-ness'), and the choice-making activity of each individual mind differs from that of all other individual minds. But that which lies behind and provokes the choice-making activity of individualized minds is a mind-stuff common to all individuals. This common mind-stuff is a very subtle product of the flow of nature. Why and how does this common mind-stuff became divided among individualized minds, and why does each of them make choices different from those of others? The answer is: when the mind appears on the scene through the temporal process of nature, and especially when it appears in the human being, it is seen to be influenced by individual choice-making and this differs from one individual to another. Obviously, therefore, something other than the temporal flow of nature has made its appearance in man. This is 'pure seeing', which makes man conscious of everything other than himself. This 'pure seeing' is also common to all individual human beings. It is because of this that an object such as a 'tree' is a tree for all human beings. This is true of all objects and of the whole objective world.

But together with 'pure seeing' something else has also appeared on the scene. This is freedom of choice. This does not belong to nature, and not, and could not be, a product of its temporal movement. This is so because what nature produces is always common to all perceivers. This is the most decisive distinguishing mark of objectivity. Therefore, something new and distinct from objectivity has appeared in man. This new and distinct thing is 'freedom'. This is what distinguishes man from the rest of creation. But although freedom is present in every man individuals tend to exercise it under the influence of the past or temporality. Man tends to identify himself (the 'seer' in him) with the ideational, subjective movement of his mind, i.e. with *vrttis*. And when he thus gets entangled in *vrtti*-

sarupya, he remains unaware of the totally free 'pure seeing', which in fact constitutes his existential identity. The whole endeavour of Yoga is to extricate man's manness from this entanglement, and establish him in his existential identity (*savrupa*).

One who has attained a right view of the existential situation, sees that the ways of *vastu* and the ways of individualized minds (*citta*) are distinct from each other (Sutra 15). He also sees that his individualized mind cannot alter the ways of *vastu* or the objective world. The latter is in no way subservient to the action which emanates from his mind. To assume that one can alter the ways of *vastu*, or the objective world which is not of one's making, and about the nature, structure and inherent operations of which one knows next to nothing is to superimpose fiction on fact. This cannot have any validity. If this be so, then what is one to do? On the one hand there is the individual mind and its operations, and on the other there are the operations of the objective world (*vastu*). How can these two ever establish a meaningful relationship with each other? This is the question posed by Sutra 16. It is the most fundamental question – the question of all questions. It cannot be answered by any individual mind indulging in any kind of ideation or guesswork for we have already seen that the ways of an individualized mind and those of *vastu* are totally different from each other.

Therefore, neither ideation, nor speculation, nor inferential, experimental or instrumental logic, in short, no *citta-vrtti* can answer this question. *Citta-vrttis* have to cease for the right answer to emerge.

Sutra 17 enbodies this right answer. It says that *citta* or the mind has an innate passion for the *vastu* or objects of the objective world. This passion (*uparaga*) is not a *vrtti*. It is an existential imperative. It is an existential necessity for the very survival of all animate beings including man. Man does not want to die. He wants to live. And to live means to live in a meaningful relationship with the objective world. That is to say, to live is to be vitally related with the objective world in a way that illuminates the existential trinity of aloneness, otherness and togetherness.

Hunger drives one to find food, thirst to find water, sex to seeks its natural satisfaction. These drives are not *vrttis* or ideational luxuries. They involve an existential imperative which hides within its womb the whole mystery of life and of existence as a whole.

Sutra 17 says that the objective world or *vastu* becomes known or remains unknown, depending upon the mind's passion for it. If there were no passion to drive man towards the objective world there would be no knowledge at all of anything at any time. True knowledge is not ideation but a passionate feeling for the meaning of life that vibrates within one for the fulfilment of hunger, thirst or sex, which an appropriate object or *vastu* offers to man. There is an existential thrill of the joy of life in this fulfilment. The existential significance of togetherness, of aloneness and otherness is illuminated by this passion and its natural fulfilment. In the absence of this, life would remain sterile and utterly meaningless.

But alas! Man ignores this existential passion and its fulfilment. He does not pause and ponder over the existential significance of such simple, innocent and natural events. His egocentric mind rides roughshod over such events and craves for more, more, and yet more. He becomes greedy, aggressive, voluptuous and vulgar. He ignores the fact that survival which necessitates experience and enjoyment of the objective world means and implies survival of all beings and not 'my survival' at the cost of everything else. And when 'my survival', 'your survival' and the 'survival of all beings and life as a whole', begin to clash with one another, the man faces nothing but sorrow, misery and an ever mounting threat to the survival of life on this earth. Therefore, when the existential and well-defined limit of individual need is crossed, this crossing turns need into greed and man into a monster.

One who sees all this and holds himself back and remains in a state of choiceless awareness of the existential situation, comes upon a new revelation which illuminates the mystery of life and existence. Sutra 18 embodies this revelation. It says that *purusa*, or the manness of man that reposes and abides in man's body, is changeless (*a-parinami*). It never undergoes any change, as the objective world always does. The objective world always offers experiences to *purusa* or man, through his senses and mind. The mind is thus stirred by its interaction with the *vastu*. This stirring serves as a stimulation to *vrttis*. And one who sees these *vrttis*, with their existential significance, knows all about their operations, even the most subtle of them. The manness in man (*purusa*) is thus always all-knowing. The *purusa* in man never allows himself to get identified with any *vrtti*. His mind (without *vrtti*) thus assumes a quiet and crystal clear transparency, reflecting all objects and indeed, the whole objective world in its existential authenticity.

When this happens, one sees that the mind (*citta*) is not self-luminous, because it has now become the 'seen', reflecting the objective world in its purity (Sutra 19). One also sees that the mind can either reflect the 'seer' or the 'seen', but cannot ascertain or determine (*avadharana*) both at one and the same time (Sutra 20). It is not the mind that 'sees' but the 'seer' who sees the mind, and, through it, the objective world. He sees the absurdity of assuming that one mind becomes an observer of the contents of another mind, and this another of yet another mind, *ad infinitum*. For instance, one experiences pain or sorrow. Who sees this pain or sorrow? The mind? If so, who wants to get rid of this pain? Another mind? If so, who seeks to find a way out? Yet another mind? – And yet another, and yet another, and so on? To see the absurdity of this is to see the existential nature of the mind as a neutral link between the 'seer' and the 'seen'. Mind ceases to be the right kind of link when man, remaining unaware of his existential manness, gets identified with the ideational movements of his mind which are invariably propelled by past impressions. So long as this situation persists, man remains unintelligent, and is swept off his feet and carried away into the whirl of events, like a log of dead wood in a raging torrent. But when this situation comes to an end, man sees all the movements of his mind as he sees the trees, or the birds or the clouds. The experiences of these objects come and go exactly as the clouds do, leaving the sky clear and unaffected. Man's manness is like this sky, within whose limitless expanse, all events in this universe take place. The *purusa*, or man's manness, remains wholly unaffected by them, although each of them gives a thrill of the joy of life and then passes away without leaving any mark of likes or dislikes on the mind-stuff. This is so because *purusa* is existentially unchangeable (*a-parinami*, Sutra 18).

Thus, when one sees the mind's *vrttis*, as one sees the clouds appearing and disappearing, one suddenly becomes aware of what intelligence (*buddhi*) means and implies (Sutra 22). To be intelligent is to be objective about all the movements of one's mind. Subjectivity is nothing but *vrtti-sarupya* (identifications with the *vrttis* of the mind). Therefore subjectivity must end for intelligence to be. It is this intelligence that enables man to see objects as they are in their existential authenticity. This is the real perception of objectivity.

Sutras 23 and 24 describe clearly what role the mind plays when perception becomes totally objective.

It is necessary here to recall what the opening four Sutras have already told us about the mind. It is pertinent to note that the Yoga

Sutras use the word *citta* to denote mind. They do not use any other synonym, such as *manas* or *antahkarana*. As we have seen, the word *citta* is derived from the root *cit*, which means 'to see, perceive, observe'. *Citta* is the past passive participle of *cit*. It signifies the accumulation of impressions of what has been seen or experienced in the past. *Citta* is thus made up of these impressions of past experiences which get imprinted on the brain cells. They carry a code of information gathered from past experiences. From the point of view of biology and the evolution of the species, this code is passed on to the individuals of a species from generation to generation. Its beginning can never be ascertained. This is what Sutras 7 to 13 also tell us; Sutra 10 in particular makes a specific reference to the beginningless characteristic of past impressions carrying a code.

The mind becomes active through the interaction that constantly goes on between the 'seer' and the 'seen' (man and the objective world). It is the very nature of the mind and the brain cells to record everything that is seen, along with the reactions generated within the mind. The records of these reactions are called *sanskaras* and these are the raw material of memory. Sutra 9 says that *smrti* (memory) and *sanskàra* (past impressions) are of the same nature.

When, as a result of the interaction constantly going on between the 'seer' and the 'seen', one sees anything interesting or arresting, what happens instantly is the stirring of the memory. As a result, one tends to understand the encounter between the 'seer' and the 'seen' in terms of the past with which one has become familiar. In this manner, the past overshadows the ever active and living present. Pure perception thus gets coloured and distorted by the past. Ideation and thought usurp the place of facts and the vicious circle of confusion between facts and fancies goes on from experience to experience and from generation to generation. We have already seen how this vicious circle can be broken and man's entanglement with it ended by the discipline of Yoga.

Sutras 23 and 24 tell us that when perception becomes pure and totally objective the mind is left still and without any movement. It becomes as neutral as a pure crystal which reflects the colours of objects brought in its vicinity and shows no trace of these colours when the objects are removed from its vicinity. This in fact is the existential quality of the mind: to reflect 'what is' in its existential purity and authenticity. It is this quality that operates when the perception is pure and totally objective. Sutra 23 says that when the mind reflects the two distinct realities – the 'seer' and the 'seen' as they are in their existential purity, it becomes inclusive of all objects (*sarvartham*). This becomes possible because *vrttis* no longer distract, disturb and distort 'what is'. The 'seer' at one end, and the 'seen' or the objective world at the other exhaust between them the whole of the universe. The mind, in a state of stillness, operates like a stainless mirror in which both the 'seer' and the 'seen' are reflected in their existential distinctness. This distinction lies in one thing only. That is, whereas the 'seen' or the objective world is temporal and ever changing, the 'seer' is non-temporal and changeless.

Sutra 24 says that the mind exists not for itself but for the benefit of something other than itself, the *purusa*. Just as objects and the objective world exist for another (*parartha*), as stated in II-18, so also mind exists for another. Everything that is put together by time exists for the other. That which is not put together by time, but which sees in a flash all that has been put together by time, exists for itself only (*svartha*). This latter is the existential nature of the 'seer'; and *citta* (mind) as we have seen is made up of impressions of past experiences. It is therefore a product of time. But *citta* differs from all the other temporal objects in one respect. Being *citta*, it carries along with it an element of *cit*; and so when the *cit*, the seeing energy of the 'seer', gets cleared of the shadows of the past, *citta* becomes pure emptiness, capable of reflecting everything. And even though this *citta* may get coloured by innumerable impressions, it still retains its existential characteristic of serving its master, the 'seer' (Sutra 18). In fact it is the existential *raison d'être* of the mind to be of assistance to the 'seer' to realize his identity (II-23).

What happens after one has completely understood the *raison d' être* of the mind and of the objective world, is described in the following Sutras which are discussed in the next chapter.

3
Freedom and Creativity

SUTRAS 25 TO 34

25. *Viśeṣadarśina ātmabhāvabhāvanā nivṛttih*

In the case of one whose vision has become uniquely discerning ideational self-indulgence centred in I-ness comes to an end.

26. *Tadā vivekanimnaṁ kaivalya-prāgbhāraṁ cittaṁ*

Then the mind tends towards objects only in the light of discerning intelligence and becomes freedom-oriented.

27. *Tacchidreṣu pratyayāntarāṇi saṅskārebhyah*

In the holes of that mind various experiences continue to linger because of past impressions.

28. *Hānameṣāṁ kleśavaduktaṁ*

They [the impressions of past experiences] should be discarded in the same way as the tensions are discarded.

29. *Prasaṅkhyāne-pyakusīdasya sarvathā vivekakhyāterdharma-meghah samādhih*

One who does not behave like a moneylender despite the plenitude of things he commands, and who remains established in discerning intelligence, attains to *Samadhi*, which is called *dharmamegha.*

30. *Tatah kleśa-karmanivṛttih*

Thereby tensions and tension-born activity come to an end.

31. *Tadā sarvāvaraṇamalānetasya jñānasyā-naṅtyājjñeyamalpaṁ*

Then little remains to be known or understood because all the impurity which covers knowingness is eliminated and knowingness becomes infinite.

32. *Tatah kṛtārthānāṁ pariṇāma-krama-samāptirguṇānāṁ*

In the case of those who have thus become totally self-fulfilled, the sequences of the cause–effect movement, triggered by the three-fold energies [*gunas*], come to an end.

33. *Kṣaṇapratiyogī pariṇāmāparānta-nirgrāhyah kramah*

Sequential movement [*krama*] is that which is perceived only after the effect is brought into being by the moments of time that have gone away. *Krama* is thus *ksanapratiyogi* [i.e. when *krama* is there *ksana* is not there.

34. *Puruṣārthaśūnyānāṁ guṇānāṁ pratiprasavah kaivalyaṁ svarūpapratiṣṭhā vā citiśakatiriti*

Creativity which runs counter to the movement of the three-fold energies [*gunas*] that have become meaningless to *purusa* [the manness of man], is called freedom, establishment in one's identity, or seeing Energy. [This is the ending of Yoga.]

NOTES AND COMMENTS

We are now approaching the end of the journey. It started with the word *atha*, and it now ends with the word *iti*. *Atha* and *iti* mean respectively the beginning and the end.

The logic of the discipline of Yoga that started with Sutra 1 ends up in creative movement that runs counter to the temporal movement of the objective world. This creative movement is called freedom (*kaivalya*). It establishes man in his existential identity, which now remains eternally charged with Seeing Energy (*citisakti*). And this is the end (*iti*) of the discipline of Yoga.

The Sutras now under consideration describe what happens when one's mind has, through the discipline of Yoga, regained its existential quality of not moving either towards the 'seer' or towards the 'seen', the two poles of the existential situation. As we have seen, the existential situation is composed of three basic factors: the 'seer', the 'seen' or the objective world, and the medium through which the 'seer' receives the objects of the objective world and thus gets related to it in the existential sense. For this relationship to be real, meaningful and totally satisfying it must always be in harmony with the existential situation. All other forms of relationships, which are for the most part conjured up by the choice-making ideational movement of the mind, are not relationships at all, but are dream-like phantoms of wishful thinking, whatever the forms they may take and whatever the social respectability they may attain.

The fundamental problem of man is therefore the problem of relationship. And since all relationships take shape only through the mind (*citta*), the Yoga Darsana concerns itself wholly with the nature and structure of the mind and its total transformation in terms of the existential situation. Transformation to be real and creative must take place in the mind of man, and nowhere else. So long as the mind remains caught up in the choice-making ideational movement, it is bound to distort the existential situation and end up in confusion, conflict, misery and chaos. The Yoga Darsana offers a way out of the tragedy to which man had become heir through his failure to see and understand his existential situation. Once this is understood, the human situation that seems oppressively restrictive in the beginning later becomes so pliable that the three-fold cosmic energies of which the world is an ever changing manifestation, as it were, offer their services to man in order to transform the existential situation through freedom and ever renewed creation.

Sutra 25 says that a man who has understood and thoroughly assimilated what has been expounded in the previous Sutras becomes a man with a new vision. This vision is unique (*visesa*) in the sense that nothing like it ever existed before; for it is a vision that transcends temporality and vibrates in a timeless dimension – within the very being of man. This vision brings to an end the sense of 'I-ness' (*atma-bhavabhavana*) and all forms of self-indulgence that are triggered by it.

Sutra 26 states that with the total elimination of self-centredness and self-indulgence, the mind acquires a totally new quality. In fact, it regains its existential purity which got corrupted through the operations of egocentricity. The mind thus liberated from all egocentric ideational perversities, becomes pure and crystal clear. Because of this, it gets charged with discerning intelligence and becomes totally freedom-oriented. To be freedom-oriented is to hold oneself back from getting entangled in the maddening whirl of temporality. This is the basic requirement for an ever fresh and ever renewing creative vision.

Even so, the natural mind-stuff is so pliable and flexible that it continues to receive impressions of various experiences. There are moments of inattention in every man's life, howsoever alert and intelligent he may be or become. These moments of inattention are like holes (*cchidra*) in the mind-stuff. They get filled by the impressions of the ever repeated experiences, as the pores of a porous substance get filled by water that is poured into them. This is what is stated in Sutra 27. And Sutra 28 says that these accumulations have to be squeezed out as often as may be necessary. It is easy to press a porous substance and squeeze out all the accumulated water from it.

But the pores of the mind can be emptied of all the impurities only in one way. It is the same way as tensions are eliminated, as indicated in Sutras 10 and 11 of Part II. This way is the way of *pratiprasava* and *dhyana* or meditation.

When this is done, one finds oneself blessed with a plenitude which is boundless. This happens because the mind that ceases to move either towards the 'seer' or towards the 'seen' and only reflects both in their existential purity becomes all-inclusive (Sutra 23). And one who does not behave like a moneylender (*kusida*) who has plenty of money, and who does not trade with this plenitude with a view to making a personal profit, but, on the other hand, shares it with all who care to participate in it and who remains wholly established in discerning intelligence acquires a qualitatively different and heightened *Samadhi*. This is given the name of *Dharma-megha Samadhi* (Sutra 29).

The word *Dharma-megha* literally means 'the cloud of cosmic order'. *Dharma*, in its ancient Vedic sense, means 'cosmic order' and *megha* means 'a cloud'. This suggests that one who lives in the way mentioned in Sutra 29 lives in total harmony with the cosmic order. It also suggests, through the word *megha*, that this supra-ordinary *Samadhi* is like a cloud full of the eternal waters of life, which is capable of pouring down and blessing the world with its immortal life-giving waters. To share what one has with others is to experience the infinite bliss of cosmic togetherness.

Sutra 30 states that the *Dharma-megha Samadhi* brings about a total negation of tensions and tension-born activity. Sutra 31 states that when tensions and tension-born activity are negated, all the coverings of impurities which cloud the mind are removed. Since mind is the only medium through which knowledge is obtained, a totally purified mind becomes capable of all-knowingness. Little remains that is knowable outside the infinite range of such a mind.

Sutra 32 describes the man with such a mind and blessed with such omniscience as a totally self-fulfilled being (*krtartha*). In respect of such a man the causative operations of the objective world come to an end. He is liberated from the prison-house of causality whose relentless wheels are kept going by the three-fold cosmic energies (*gunas*).

Sutra 33 explains *karma* or the sequences of causality. It says that causality is temporal. Time is an ever continuing sequence of moments (*ksana*). It is so subtle that no one can observe it. It never becomes the 'seen'. But an accumulated effect, caused by these sequences of moments, becomes visible as an object, and hence cognizable. From this cognition one infers that this object is the result of the sequence of many moments that have passed away, never to return. The effect is thus a product of a series of unseen moments which we call by the name 'time'. When the effect (*parinama*) in the form of an object is there the moments of time that produced it are not. Hence an effect is described in the Sutra as the opposite (*pratiyogi*) of *ksana* or time. This time is one-dimensional. All three-dimensional objects are the products of time, which in fact is a series of discrete moments. Measurable time and measurable space are the illusions of a mind which is caught up in past impressions kept active by memory. These measures of time and space can never offer a solution to the riddle of the universe, even at the purely physical level; for time itself is the riddle, and time is wholly internal, invisible and uncognizable, never lending itself to measure. A measure-oriented mind is incapable of comprehending the immeasurable, which is time as the swift-moving and subtle sequences of unobservable moments. These sequences, according to Yoga, are triggered by the interplay of the three-fold cosmic energies, mentioned in II-18. And mind also is the product of these three-fold energies, a product with a unique quality which is capable of offering experiences of the objective world to man, the 'seer'. Therefore, it is the mind whose operations have to be inquired into and thoroughly understood before anything else can ever be rightly understood. This is what Yoga Darsana does throughout these Sutras.

One who has made the journey so far, in the sense in which the Sutras expect one to do, comes to a point where the existential nature of the objective world stands revealed before his eyes. It is a world governed by time and causality whose subtle operations now hold no mystery for the Yogic eye. As soon as this happens the cosmic energies that maintain the world begin to offer all their powers to the Yogic to whom, however, they can in fact offer nothing new or meaningful as their very *raison d'être* has ended so far as the Yogi is concerned. They therefore begin to run counter to their one-dimensional temporality and through the Yogi become creative. This is called *pratiprasava* in Sutra 34. One whose every presence turns the temporal cosmic energies into an ever fresh creativity in total freedom is said to be established in his existential identity. This identity is also known as *citi-sakti* or Seeing Energy.

So long as the 'seen' dominates man's vision, the Seeing Energy remains dormant and inactive. But the moment man realizes that he is the 'seer' and looks at the 'seen', the latter becomes an instrument of his ever renewed creativity.

This is where Yoga ends, in the creation of a new mind, a new man and a new world. Yoga thus opens up infinite possibilities of bliss and beatitude for mankind through the awakening of Seeing Energy, which is eternally free and infinitely creative of that which is pregnant with Truth, Goodness and Beauty.